Osebol

MARIT KAPLA

Osebol

Voices from a Swedish Village

Translated by PETER GRAVES

ALLEN LANE
an imprint of
PENGUIN BOOKS

ALLEN LANE

UK | USA | Canada | Ireland | Australia
India | New Zealand | South Africa

Allen Lane is part of the Penguin Random House group of companies
whose addresses can be found at global.penguinrandomhouse.com

First published in Swedish by Teg Publishing 2019
This translation published in Penguin Books 2021

001

Set in 10/13.5pt Warnock Pro
Typeset by Jouve (UK), Milton Keynes
Printed and bound in Great Britain by Clays Ltd, Elcograf S.p.A.

The authorized representative in the EEA is Penguin Random House Ireland,
Morrison Chambers, 32 Nassau Street, Dublin D02 YH68

A CIP catalogue record for this book is available from the British Library

ISBN: 978–0–241–53520–2

www.greenpenguin.co.uk

To all those who live, have lived and will live in Osebol

NORWAY

Klarälven

Sysslebäck

Branäs
Malung
Ambjörby
Likenäs
Osebol
Stöllet
Ekshärad
Torsby

Oslo

Stockholm

Karlstad
Örebro

Gothenburg

SWEDEN

DENMARK

Baltic Sea

Copenhagen
Malmö

GERMANY
POLAND

0   100   200 miles
0   100   200   300 km

Let me tell you something . . .
my life has been like Värmland.

Mountains and valleys.

It's had its ups and its downs.

We moved here with everything we owned.

Me and a mate
came in the lorry
and Tina and the children
in the ordinary car.

It was two or three degrees below zero
when we arrived at the house.

It was at the end of September
or the beginning of October.

Just before the start of the elk hunting season.

The Milky Way lay
like a starry barrier across the sky.

I had this buzz in my ears all the time.

Can't you hear it, too?
I said and went outside
where our electric meter was on a pole
with a load of overhead wires and the like.

Then eventually I realised . . .
what I was hearing was silence
something I hadn't heard for twenty years
in Stockholm.

I think you appreciate it more
the longer you've been away.

I can see
there are days when it's magnificent
but otherwise . . .

For me, it's just
a bloody valley
sort of.

Looking out
of the upstairs window
at Klarastrand

I saw a salmon
swimming
just below the surface.

How silly of me!

We could easily have drunk coffee out of the cups
the doctor drank his coffee from
when Alf was born.

I've still got them.

I get them out
for special occasions
but I always say
Watch you don't break them.

Linda cares about things like that, too
and wants to hang on to the old things
that have always been around.

How old would Alf have been now?

Ninety-three.

They must be at least a hundred years old, these cups.

He was a big baby
and they had to send for the doctor.

He was born in a room upstairs.

Arne was christened here.

Finnsson and Ebba came.

Alf went and fetched them.

He owned a new Chevy.

He was running a taxi at the time.

The minister was really taken aback
when he arrived in a different car.

I'd made a tart topped with wild strawberries.

East of here by the river
there were so many wild strawberries at the field's edge.

There used to be more wild strawberries
than we get now.

They were everywhere.

Alf did his national service
with a fellow from Gothenburg.

He was in the cavalry
horses
and he could never understand
how the Gothenburg man
ended up in the cavalry.

He knew nothing about horses.

Alf said to him
Have you ever had anything
to do with horses?

No, he said
I may have seen an occasional nag in the square now and again.

Then the fellow asked
about Alf's job.

Well, forestry worker.

Oh, he said
enjoyable
and good for your health.

That's what Alf used to say
when you had to wade through snow
up to your knees.

The man knew nothing at all
about forestry work.

What was that? How did I end up meeting Alf?

I was working in Torsby at the time
in the kitchen
of the Café Company.

They served food and beer there.

I went to a dance in Ambjörby
one Boxing Day
and that's where I met Alf.

Then at the start
we sort of got together every now and then.

We got married in the March of nineteen fifty
though I'd moved here in forty-nine.

I stopped working
and I've lived here ever since.

North of us is Alvar's field
Hemgårn.

South of us used to be Bengt's
but the fellow at Eftnäs has it now
he came into it after Bengt.

After that it's Per-Erik.

Then comes Nystuga
and everything belonging to it
all the land.

Over to the east is Törnsgårn
over by the bridge.

There are no more fields after that.

The soil here is very sandy
and potatoes like it like that, you know.

We used to plant them in spring
and lift them in autumn.

We've got a root cellar
where we kept the potatoes.

They'd keep until the next harvest.

Then I'd have to have a throw-out
and clean the cellar.

That's what you do.

We didn't have any animals
when I came here
except the pigs in the summer
but no cows or horses
or anything.

They'd had them here before.

But then along comes
this woman
who wasn't a real farmer's wife.

I had nothing to do with all that
I was just a posh lady.

Then along came Arne.

He was my job from then on.

And I had to stay at home.

He came home from school once.

Eivor and I were out in the forest
and hadn't got home in time.

And he said
You know what
he said
You have to be at home
when I come home.

He was seven
and had just started school.

I mustn't not be there.

Eivor lived at her parents' place
at Eftnäs.

They built above the shop later
at about the same time as we moved
into this house.

I didn't know her before that.

She's always lived in this valley.

It was through the children.

We saw one another at the maternity clinic . . .

Mona and Arne
are the same age.

We used to meet quite often.

Then more and more often
as we got older.

Then there was berry picking.

God knows how many berries we picked.

When you went into the forest it was red everywhere.

It was lovely out in the forest.

We used a berry scoop
and went along picking
with big baskets on our backs
thirty kilograms in weight.

We'd fill them
take them to the car
and go and fetch another one.

It put money in our pockets.

We could get as much as eighteen, nineteen kronor a kilo.

You wouldn't get that now.

Not bad money.

We wanted that bit extra, you see.

When you finished school in those days
you had to go and find a job.

I couldn't have been more than sixteen or seventeen.

Dad had a cousin down in Åtorp
who'd converted an old manor house
into a guest house.

She phoned Dad
around the time I was ready to leave home.

Dad took me to Torsby on his bike
and put me on the train.

There I was
never been anywhere before.

I had to change in Kil
to get to Kristinehamn.

That's where this cousin Fia was going to meet me.

I'd never seen her
and she'd never seen me.

I stayed there for some time
helping her with the food and the cleaning
and anything to do with running a guest house.

She was kind to me.

It was a good start.

But then Mum wasn't well
and I had to come home.

They needed help at home
and I had to do my bit.

That's how it goes.

There were a couple of old women
Maja and Maria
living at Tôrkhushia
where Jan and Lotten live now.

I went and helped them quite a bit.

She used to say
the wife of the man there, I mean
You're a kind of home help, you are.

But in the end they went into Klarastrand too
the care home.

Maja was Maria's husband's sister.

She was a bit senile
or how should I put it
she was a little bit strange.

She'd been to help with the baking
over at Törnsgårn
then she passed by here.

She'd rolled up
the apron she was wearing.

She had a loaf in it
she'd been given to take home.

I was at home the whole time.

Never went out to work.

I was a housewife.

Then I started part-time at the Folk High School
and ended up full-time there.

In the kitchen.

I've always been in a kitchen.

They used to divide up elk meat out in the barn.

There could be as many as sixty or so elk hunters
wanting coffee
and sandwich cake too, sometimes.

It was all go.

I enjoyed that
after coming back home without a job.

It was hard going
when I was at the Folk High School.

You'd get home
and the place was full of meat
you had to deal with.

It wasn't always easy.

But I was young and healthy then.

Now I'm just young.

There used to be a market in Osebol years ago
that's why they started one up again.

We ran a lottery to support the Stödalen ski slope.

We went around begging for prizes,
wove rugs and so on . . .
otherwise Stödalen wouldn't have come off.

Nothing comes to anything
if people won't pitch in and help.

They had to have electricity
for a lighted ski trail.

No one goes there any longer
now there's no electricity.

We had rationing, of course,
on food and coffee.

Anyone with a farm
got by all right, though.

They had food.

But they had to inform the people
who issued the ration cards
if they slaughtered
a pig or a calf.

You couldn't just polish off
however much you wanted.

It had to go on the card, you see.

Other people got coupons
to buy meat in the shop.

We've been spared the wars
suffered by the countries round us.

We've just sort of sat here, we have.

But we've certainly got a lot of foreigners.

If there's room for them, why not?

They need help.

But the people still left there need help, too.

Perhaps even more.

It's horrifying
the way the world is these days.

People say
the world is upside down
and it is.

Endless injustice
and war after war.

Wouldn't it be wonderful
if everyone could just come together and agree.

But that was back in the old days.

Maybe it wasn't really like that
but we didn't get to hear about everything then
the way we do now.

The media.

They talk about everything now.

This is the almond cake
I made this week.

I just thought one day
I'm blowed if I'm not going to give it a try.

I can't manage to bake white bread these days.

I can't stand for that long
what with my back.

But doing this I can sit and beat it
over by the worktop.

I can manage that.

I've made lots of them.

I used to take them to sell at the market in Osebol.

All this forest
trees, trees, trees, trees
animals you won't find in Denmark
and a completely different climate.

We have a canoe
that we use on the river
to watch beavers
and fish.

Sometimes we come across a sandy island
out in the river.

We stay there all day
and only go home in the evening.

We spent every third week here
when my wife was ill.

Every time she'd been given
chemotherapy
we came here
because the air is better.

The moss that grows on the trees
the sort that looks like a beard
can only grow
where the air is rich in oxygen.

If there isn't sufficient oxygen
it can't grow.

We notice a difference
compared with Denmark.

When we come up here
we sleep.

We sleep deeply
with the windows open
to let the wind blow in.

The chap who used to own the house
his name was Holger Andersson.

He was a bus driver who lived in Karlstad
and came up here in the summer . . .
every summer as long as I can remember, old bloke.

They wanted to sell the place in nineteen ninety.

I grew up just next door.

I always said
I'd buy that house
if he decided to sell
because I thought, it's got such a good position.

So I bought it.

He'd come up every summer.

Plant potatoes in the field.

He had one of those old-fashioned hand ploughs
with wooden shafts.

You had to pull it for him
and be like a little horse.

I hated it I can tell you.

Time to come and pull my plough.

I wasn't that old.

I thought it was a real pain.

But apart from that Holger was harmless.

They were mission people, religious.

I work in Örebro these days
so I leave here
at four o'clock Monday morning
and leave Örebro at four on Thursday evening.

We work forty hours on site
so the days are long.

We work till eight every evening
and live in a hotel.

But that's life, isn't it?

There are no jobs up here.

So there's not a lot of choice.

It's really hard to get people.

There aren't any building workers
without jobs these days
so we've brought in loads of Estonians.

They're really good workers
no doubt about that
but only two of them can manage any English
the rest can't speak a word.

They aren't easy to communicate with
and it's not as if my English
is the best in the world, anyway.

Not being able to talk to them makes things difficult.

The men who built the ski lodge up at Branäs last year . . .
they were Estonians, all of them.

It was built of modules
shipped over from Estonia.

It was presumably much cheaper to do that
though they could have got them from Torsby
which is only about twenty-five miles away.

Price is what decides everything, of course.

Why choose a Moelven product
in Torsby or Karlstad or Säffle
when they can be manufactured in Estonia
shipped over and assembled here.

It must be a good deal cheaper to do that.

Say half the price
or maybe seventy-five percent.

They're obviously going to choose what's cheapest.

It must have been eighty-eight, eighty-nine when it got started.

That's when they built the top and bottom stations for the lift.

Then came the two cabin villages down in the valley
and two at the top.

After that everything just came to a standstill.

Nothing happened for many years.

It must have been about fifteen years ago it got going again.

When new owners took over.

The development really took off then.

The valley's lucky to have Branäs
otherwise there'd be virtually nothing.

Especially since the chipboard factory closed down
where quite a few people used to work.

Otherwise there's not a lot to choose from up here.

The world has always been in a hurry
but I think it's going that way more and more.

And then you're getting older, too
can't keep up the same pace
you once did.

When you're at home on Fridays
you're tired
no question about it.

Fridays are spent
just resting and doing nothing.

You don't have the energy
to do anything very useful.

We've been thinking about this a bit.

I don't think today's youngsters
will do this kind of work in the future.

Not when you can sit at a computer
and earn a lot more
without having to do work
that makes you filthy.

I don't think they will, I don't.

Getting worn-out and tired.

I don't think so.

Youngsters today and their mobiles.

We've had some younger ones.

You know what it's like . . .
they've got to be on the phone
every minute.

It's not on.

But that's how it is.

They can't live without their mobiles.

It's a disease these days and they've all caught it.

They have to have a phone and stay in the loop.

Everything is a priority.

Pushed for time.

Things are supposed to be finished
before they're even started.

We're a couple of weeks behind schedule
in Örebro.

It's supposed to be finished
by the date set for inspection.

Same in Stockholm and everywhere else.

By the inspection date.

That's when it has to be ready.

They have to find the workers
but there aren't any Swedes available
so they'll have to employ casuals.

That means Estonians.

Everything's architect-designed these days.

That seems to be the fashion.

Orange facade
orange and grey.

Orange is sort of . . .
well, it's not a colour I'd choose.

But it's architect-designed.

They're going to have to change things a bit
otherwise everything will look the same.

Bright orange really makes your house stick out.

But the people who move in
seem pleased with it.

These days chipboard isn't used
as much as it used to be.

We used to use chipboard for floors
and chipboard for walls.

There'll come a time when you won't see it at all
in the building trade.

It's other materials now, plaster and the like.

Of course, it's a by-product.

Sawdust from the sawmills.

They used to not pay a penny for it.

But then came pellets
made of it.

And up went the price
as more people were prepared to pay for it.

The worst thing is you suddenly end up
having to pay for a by-product
you used to get for nothing.

So production costs become more expensive.

There's nothing wrong with chipboard.

It's a good material to use.

It's good to work with.

But it is wood, after all.

And if you use chipboard panels on a wall
they'll dry out and the joins will show.

That never happens
when you use plasterboard
because it's a dead material.

Chipboard is wood
and it still has life in it.

Everyone up here . . .
you could get it for next to nothing
as long as you knew someone there.

They used to cut for IKEA, too
bookshelves and furniture.

But nothing more was done
after they built it, the factory.

Eventually the machines became ancient.

I think that's part of the reason
they invested in Östersund . . .
the gear up there was more up to date.

They'd been talking about it for years.

I could see the way things were going
and I wasn't surprised.

It's a pity for the schools and all that
given the knock-on effect.

Fewer job opportunities
mean fewer people.

The more people the better
for the schools and shops.

That's obvious.

Osebol gets livelier in the summer.

That's when everyone comes
like my neighbours there.

There's more of a buzz then.

Very little happens during the winter.

For my part, though,
being away all week and working so hard . . .

Fridays and Saturdays
and Sundays
when I'm at home
I don't want to go out to anything.

There's some concern about
how much longer the school can survive.

Ida will get to stay right through
but after that . . .
the classes are getting so small.

Can't be more than twenty-five counting all the classes.

They can't carry on like that, can they.

Ebba did Years Seven, Eight and Nine in Torsby.

She found it hard going.

Had to get up so early.

And she's not very keen on going by bus.

My mum lives in Torsby
and she stayed with her quite a lot.

We've got a flat for her now
so she doesn't have to travel.

We'll have to see whether Ida will stay there too
once she starts.

I went to school in Karlstad.

Me and Dennis down the way started there.

We rented rooms.

I'm sure we could have got places at Torsby
but we thought it would be fun
to be in the town.

I don't think it was a mistake.

You learned to stand on your own two feet.

When I left school I did seven months in the army.

After that I got a job and worked for a while.

Then they were looking for people up in Ransby.

So I thought bugger it
I'd rather be at home.

I suppose I'm stubborn and will stay here.

I don't know why.

I've said it might have been better
to have moved away right off.

But I'm stubborn as a pig and will stay.

I don't really get on in a city anyway.

I don't want to be stuck on some bloody housing estate.

That's not my thing at all.

I'd rather potter about at home.

It can be a bit tough.

The weeks are long when you have to work away from home.

And you're not getting any younger.

But that's how things are.

You want to get back to Osebol, of course.

It's a kind of disease.

There must be something that explains it.

Maybe it's because I grew up here.

That must be it.

But numbers are shrinking.

I used to have a lot to do with Arne
after all, we were cousins.

But then he died.

Dad died the year before.

That was two thousand and eleven.

So the numbers are going down.

No one is living there.

It is mine, though.

My father used to live there.

I'm going to turn it into a garage.

Over by that open door
I'm going to put in a second door.

That'll be my job for the summer.

It was built in sixty-three
and the drainage was bad.

I had to fix it two years ago.

As to the roof . . . I had to re-roof it
last year.

Houses in Stöllet . . .
you won't get your money back.

I'll use it as an outhouse
as a garage.

To store bits and pieces and rubbish.

That'll be it.

I doubt anyone will ever move in
so I'll leave it as it is.

Many of the people round here travel away to work.

I'm used to being on my own during the week.

The time passes quickly, I think.

Monday to Thursday.

It does.

And now there's a chance he'll be at Branäs by autumn
which means he'll be able to come home.

And I've got a permanent job.

There's a shortage of teachers.

They can't get hold of anyone for supply work.

It's really difficult.

They advertised a social studies post
in Ekshärad, Years Seven to Nine.

Not a single applicant.

That's the situation.

The bus goes so early that
Ebba's found a little room with a kitchenette.

It's not the length of the journey
only thirty-five, forty minutes
just that it goes so early.

Leave the house at half past six.

It'll be the same for Ida later.

I think it's been really hard, it really has.

We'll have to see what we can work out.

We've tried lobbying
for a later bus to school
without success.

It's the school that makes the contract
which means the council, of course.

It leaves from Värnäs at ten to seven
that's what they're looking at
but everyone lives some distance from there.

She got up at half past four
in order to get ready.

Well, we'll have to see what we can work out.

It's all happened very quickly.

There aren't any children being born here.

Our pool of youngsters isn't being topped up.

Jobs are what's needed
if people are to stay.

But I don't know
what kind of jobs they could be.

In the upper years I think they can take the bus.

No question about that.

Many do.

But until Year Five or Six
they should have somewhere closer to home.

That's what happens in Ekshärad.

Some of my Year Ones catch the seven fifteen bus
and arrive at eight.

They've got a long journey
but the bus arrives just in time for start of school
and leaves for home when we finish.

If that was done I think more people would move here.

If you live in the city
and choose a school at the other end of town
you'd still be travelling for an hour.

It's not so much how long it takes
it's the early hour.

She thinks it will be great.

It feels really good.

We talked about Karlstad to begin with.

Pretty well everyone is going there these days
it's the trend.

We said
No, it's too far
given that it's not for a particular course.

Torsby's in easy reach, though
if something should happen.

They do want to get into something.

And some of them
are looking for particular courses.

Year Nine at Ekshärad now . . .
half would choose Hagfors
and half would move away.

I feel sorry for the upper secondary schools up here.

Ebba and Ida are forever saying
We'd like to have neighbours in the white house.

We'd rather not have any, though.

It's a pity it's standing empty
but there are summer visitors, after all.

The fact that it's quiet
and not having people too close
I think that's what's so good.

Of course, it's always nice
when a family with children moves in.

Actually that is happening.

Things aren't standing completely still.

But it's slower
when it comes to younger families.

You can understand
why they're reluctant . . .
given that the school isn't . . .
no one knows how long.

You can understand it.

It's occurred to us recently
there's not enough going on here
for the children.

There's plenty for us, though.

This is how we want it.

They can decide for themselves later on where they want to go.

Because there's just too few children and friends.

Living here is wonderful
that's not the problem.

The problem is the logistics.

There was a house just north of Bränna.

It had been built with three walls
and the fourth side
set into the hill.

Into the slope.

                    It was my mother's father who built it.

                              It was just a wee cottage.

                                        Brôthia
                              Bråtheden, I mean.

Mum had two brothers
Pelle and Holger.

Holger died when he was thirteen, fourteen years old.

He died of appendicitis.

                              He'd gone off to school
                    and came home in the evening.

                                    It was in Osebol
            he'd been given a lift by one of the Hemgårn people.

                              He stopped at Nygård
                    and Holger got out of the car.

                              It went without saying
                         he got out there, he did
                                   and ran home.

                              But then he died.

The following day he came out
when I was on the way to school.

                                    The man who'd given him a lift?

Yes, he came out to me and said . . .
I guess he was that ill after all.

There were tears in his eyes.

If only he'd told me, he said,
that he had pains in the belly
I'd have driven him
but he just got out when he . . .

Well, I was on the way to school
I couldn't say much to him.

It's something I'll never forget.

When we lived up at the croft
I didn't have anyone to play with.

There were two boys and a girl at Bränna
but they were so strict over there
that the girl was never allowed to visit me.

She wasn't allowed to go anywhere
no, her granny was the one who decided
what went on at Bränna.

Later I used to run down to Osebol myself
and play with the children there.

Edla never played with me.

And then you became a Spirella corsetiere.

She sold Spirella.

That's bras and corsets.

Lots of people came here
in order to try on Spirella.

They'd sit like this . . . wait.

First of all they had to stand like this . . .
and then they had to sit down . . .
and then they had to bend over like this . . .
all to see what the measurements were.

I thought it was really funny.

Dad . . .
when they'd been out somewhere and come home
he'd say
I saw someone
who could do with a Spirella.

When you go to the forest
to pick lingonberries
it's like playing the lottery.

Karin over at Byggninga and me . . .
it's such a long time ago
that it's alright to talk about it.

The land . . . forest . . . belonged to Törnsgårn
and there was us walking along the road
both of us with big baskets on our backs
when we bumped into a fellow from Törnsgårn.

Someone must have treated him
to a drink, I reckon.

He had a big field of lingonberries.

You won't believe how many lingonberries there were.

There he was and he just laughed . . .
Yes, you can pick them he said.

So we went and picked them.

We spent the whole day picking
went there a second day and I think
it was on the third day that he came.

We'd more or less picked the lot by then.

We said to ourselves
Wonder if he's going to be angry.

But he turned out not to be
and just laughed at us.

                              He must have been expecting
                              the two of you to pick the lot.

                              I think that's what he'd been expecting.

Picking lingonberries . . .
you didn't need to clean them or anything
just chuck them in the basket.

Easy as that.

And it wasn't difficult to sell them
in those days.

The old man, my dad . . .
think how many berries he must have picked.

Not that there was a lot of choice.

He worked in the forest in the winter, my dad.

He was a lumberjack, Dad was.

Do you know there used to be a house
south of Sandvik?

Up on the hill.

It burned down.

The road must be overgrown by now.

That's where Carina lived with her mum and dad
Tore and Ulla-Britt Emilsson.

It was divided into two apartments.

They lived upstairs
and Tore's brother Erland lived on the bottom floor.

I used to go home with Carina sometimes
and we'd dance to Tommy Steele.

We used to cycle to school
across the bridge.

In the winter our parents paid
for us to go on the school bus.

We used to stand and wait for it
down by the shop.

We had to cycle to school
right from when we started.

They wouldn't let children do that these days.

There's more traffic now, of course
but just think about it.

We were allowed to go by bike . . . imagine that.

There wasn't any alternative.

I work at Klarastrand Old People's Home.

We work two nights on
and then we're off for four.

I've been working there for many years.

It suits me.

But there's a lot of admin
which has become absolutely central.

Everything has to be written up
and entered on the computer.

It would be nice, it really would,
to be told now and again
Put all that to one side
and just sit down with the old people.

At one time, I tell you
we had to record every time
we went into someone's room.

We were supposed to write down
what we did
and what they did.

That's twenty-three people
and you go in and out several times.

The only thing we didn't have to make a note of
was which foot
we put through the door first.

Think of the effort it takes
when we could be spending it
with people.

On one occasion we had five sheets
A4, both sides
that we'd written
about one person
in one night.

Who's going to remember
what's on all those sheets?

My dad had been taken by the Russians.

He'd been in a Gestapo prison first.

He was the sort
that can't keep their mouths shut.

He was held by Hitler
forty-four to forty-five.

He came home before the end of the war
sometime in January.

Many decent people
were put in prison
in Hitler's Germany.

We often entertained guests at our house
and not all of these cheery guests
were very trustworthy.

My father would sit there and say
Thank God
it'll soon be over.

I heard on the BBC
that the Western front was
a total shambles.

Listening to the BBC
was absolutely strictly forbidden.

He kept his wireless
in a room next to the potato cellar.

My father had to swallow his words.

He wasn't called up, you know.

He'd been in the First World War
when he was really young
and he had three estates to look after.

The business of food production
was vital for Hitler
so Dad was exempt from military service.

Later on after Germany was divided
we lived in the part known as the DDR
or East Germany.

Where the large River Elbe is.

We lived twenty-five miles east of the Elbe.

The Americans arrived first.

They reached the Elbe long before the Russians but then they waited.

They didn't cross it.

That was a great, great pity.

I remember when they entered our little town
it's called Putlitz, that town.

It was an old medieval town
with cobbles.

The district where we lived . . .
our property
was right on the edge.

We had quite a big house.

The town was full of refugees
coming from the east.

We had taken in a good few of them.

They stayed up at night
waiting . . .
my parents
along with the rest of them.

They were so certain
it would be
the Americans who came.

They were in a cheerful mood.

If I know him
my father will definitely have produced
some bottles of champagne.

He was always so optimistic.

He went out . . .
opened a window, I think.

Then we heard it.

They came into our park
with horses.

He came back
his face deathly pale
and said
It's the Russians.

They're speaking Russian.

That's when Dad made himself scarce.

He hid with the Poles
who lived in the house across the road.

I was told this by a girl who'd lived there
when I met her later, here in Sweden.

We didn't know where he was.

Given the situation all the men had to go into hiding.

There was nothing else you could do
if you didn't want to be killed.

Everybody liked him
high and low
but he was no friend of the communists
nor of the Russians
nor of Hitler . . .
he was just an ordinary man.

There were many women who adored Hitler.

When you went to the pictures
that was the sort of film being shown.

Goebbels
who was the propaganda minister
knew what he was doing.

My mother had
two younger sisters.

They just kept on
Hitler, Hitler
all the time.

My father saw it all coming.

There was once when the girls were fifteen, sixteen
and allowed to join the adults at the table
in the dining room
which we never got to do.

They kept on and on about Hitler.

Then Dad said
If I hear that word once more
you'll find yourselves out weeding the garden.

We were forced to leave our house.

My mother had to go into hiding too.

We went to my grandmother's estate
about ten miles away.

We had a pony and cart
which we drove into the blueberry wood
and spent the night there.

There weren't any blueberries there, though
since it was only May.

After moving to my grandmother's
we were able to go back home later.

They'd wrecked the house indoors.

Putting it all straight again
was unbelievably hard work.

One night my father was taken by the Russians
because they thought he had been hiding weapons.

There was a Russian officer
an interpreter and an ordinary soldier.

They came into the bedroom where we were sleeping.

We were allowed to say goodbye to our father
and then they left.

That was October forty-seven.

It was the last time.

After being locked up under Hitler he came back.

I'll never forget that.

He came walking down the road from the railway station
with his rucksack.

I can see him
as though it were yesterday.

Afterwards, when he never came back . . .

One thought
He must surely be on the way home by now
and went to try to meet him.

They came again just before Christmas forty-seven.

They always came around five in the morning.

It was about weapons again.

Someone had reported us.

People were forever reporting all sorts of things.

It made no difference whether they were true or untrue.

We had to go with them to the garden shed.

The weapons were supposed to be up in the loft
but of course they weren't.

My mother stayed below
guarded with a submachine gun
what's it called . . . Kalashnikov
and I went up with them.

Of course, there was no chance
she'd try to run away
while I was in danger.

It doesn't seem quite so awful to you
when you're ten years old.

A bit unpleasant and exciting, rather.

We went back to the house.

He says that my mother
has to go with him.

She says
What am I to do with my three children?

Then he said . . .

Well, Russian officers
were quite charming people.

They were cultured.

They often came from an aristocratic background
quite a way back, of course
but all the same
there was something really nice about them.

He asked
whether she had any family in the West.

Yes, she said
There's my mother-in-law and my parents.

He said
In that case I'll give you twenty-four hours
to take the children there
and then come back.

He knew she wouldn't.

The interpreter got really angry.

He was a German communist.

He didn't want us to get away
but that officer was a good man
I must say.

My aunt had loads of American cigarettes.

She arranged transport for us.

We went all the way to Berlin by lorry.

From there an international train
called the Allied train
crossed the zones on its way to Hamburg.

We got to Hanover first
and that's where we saw the last of our suitcases.

You'll never believe what the railway station
was like.

So many people.

When the trains arrived
everyone just stormed forward
trying to get aboard.

It's just as well our cases were stolen.

My sister had been afraid.

She thought we'd already got on the train.

She'd fallen behind.

Suddenly we heard over the loudspeakers
that a little girl had come
to the railway mission.

So my mother . . .
stupidly or not, there's no way of knowing . . .
took us children by the hand and went there.

Meanwhile, of course,
our cases were stolen.

Obviously.

But we'd never have made it onto the train
with cases.

You can imagine what it was like . . .
a woman with three children
and two large cases
in that bedlam.

Eventually we received an invitation
from Aunt Rigmor in Sweden
who was the aunt of one of my mother's friends.

The first thing we noticed
was how clean Sweden was.

And how undamaged.

And no one stole anything.

We took the train from Hamburg across Denmark
and arrived in Nässjö.

It was night time
and we had a long wait in Nässjö.

There were shelters of a sort
where you could spend the night
and we just left our things where they were.

We didn't have much more than two cases.

We left them out on the platform all night.

It didn't even enter their heads there
that they might be stolen.

So we got to Vimmerby.

It was February.

The nineteenth of February.

I'll never forget it.

Deep snow everywhere.

Aunt Rigmor had arranged a taxi
but the taxi didn't have room for us girls.

Mummy, our luggage and our brother
got to ride in the Vimmerby taxi.

Our family had seven estates.

Still have seven estates.

After all, they do still exist.

Some people have bought theirs back.

It was impossible
to get anything back without paying.

Just couldn't be done.

Our house has been completely renovated
by someone
with plenty of money.

It really is first-class now
but it's some sort of conference centre.

I didn't have any qualifications as a language teacher
but just kept applying time after time.

Eventually I got a job in Stöllet.

We moved here and lived at the dental surgery.

That was the summer of sixty-six
and there's not much of interest after that.

I've lived here ever since
and the rest isn't worth talking about.

Boring
or tedious
but wonderful for all that.

In eighty-three I started planting trees in the forest.

We had to go way up into the hills.

It was very steep.

You had a sack full of plants.

Which you had to carry.

We had fifty spruce saplings with their roots
and we had to prepare the ground
and plant them.

Outside the planting season
it was a case of signing on the dole.

I went on a six-month tourist course.

You were supposed to have German at the end of it
but I didn't need to attend that bit
since I could already speak German.

I had to do some practical training
And that's when I came to Hotel Värmlandsporten.

I was put in the reception but I said
If you don't have any objection
I'd prefer to work nights
because we don't have time to get anything done during the day.

There's so much going on
and in reception it's just chaos.

I'd never worked nights
but it turned out all right.

I worked nights there for six years.

Then they went bankrupt.

Armgard zu Putlitz b. 1937 | *121*

He was badly tortured.

I found that out later
not very long ago.

I'd traced a man and arranged to meet him
when I was in Germany in two thousand and three.

He'd been fifteen or sixteen
at the time he met my father.

There were four of them in a cell
in the Stasi prison at Bautzen.

He could hardly bear
to meet us
since we had our own special memories of our father
and what he looked like
and what he was like.

He thought it would be dreadful to destroy all that for us.

Have you heard of Bautzen?

It's a town in Saxony in East Germany.

A very beautiful medieval town, actually.

How I hated that name
I hated that name
I hated that name.

Gustav and I went there together in two thousand and three.

I said
We'll have to go to Bautzen.

I want to see the place
where he was tortured so badly and died.

I can't get it out of my mind unless we do.

There was a huge mound there
where many, many corpses lay.

Prisoners who'd just been thrown there
and covered with soil.

They didn't have graves, nothing.

There was a small white memorial chapel.

A girl of my age
the same age as me
had placed a memento there
on which she'd written for her father
exactly what I felt for my father.

It became a symbol to me.

Bautzen and I have made peace since then.

It was an enormous building
and like most prisons
there's a balcony running around the inside
you might have seen it at the cinema
so that you can see all the way down the middle.

One day Russian soldiers
took my father
up to the topmost landing.

The rest of the prisoners
including these boys
were all standing down below
and then they saw . . .

There was a net
spread across this central space.

It was a big square area
but he'd picked out a spot
not covered by the net.

Suddenly they realised
that now . . .
he was planning to jump
and he did.

He lay on the ground screaming
and wasn't dead.

It must have been dreadful for those boys
who had seen such a lot of him.

I don't want to think about it
but since I have to tell you . . .

Then they killed him.

My sister and brother-in-law insist
that we mustn't say
he committed suicide
because he didn't
they killed him.

I do understand them.

To some people there's something shameful about it.

That's not how I see it.

I think he was brave.

He was never the same after that, that man.

He didn't want to stay in contact.

He said to me . . .
I'm just not up to it.

And I can understand that.

Such a young boy.

That prison
was known as the Yellow Misery.

Gelbe Elend.

Notorious in Germany.

Everyone forgets now.

It's a long time ago.

All those memories are slipping away.

We've never received official confirmation
or anything.

Not even that he was there
nothing of that kind.

Nor were they allowed to disclose anything.

Not until many years after the reunification.

Before that I'd have never got a word
out of that lad.

They'd had to swear
they'd never disclose anything.

I can't be angry with individuals
but I hate communism
I hate Nazism
I hate Islamism
all -isms.

I am immensely happy to be here.

There's nowhere in the whole world
more peaceful.

My brothers and sisters live completely different lives.

My sister and her husband
live in a house of their own
by the lakes in Potsdam.

And my brother and sister-in-law
live their own lives.

I would die
if I had to live that sort of life
with all those antiques
all that silver to be polished
all the people you have to socialise with
and invite to your house.

I would die.

Sitting here on my own with my dogs
that's just perfect.

Perfect all year round.

I'm forever longing for autumn to come
so I can pick berries.

But I've realised that I'm not up to
walking far now.

And I've got lost a couple of times.

I buy berries sometimes.

But I really have to go into the forest.

We always go into the forest.

Pia died last autumn
or rather
I had to have her put to sleep.

She was sixteen years old
give or take a few days.

She couldn't see any more
and she couldn't hear.

The vet, who's Dutch, said
Haven't you thought
that maybe it's time to let her go?

I said
I haven't been thinking about anything else all night
but I didn't want to be the one to suggest it.

I was glad she was the one who said it.

So we did it.

She said
Do you want to take her home with you?

I said
No.

I took a photo of her
sitting on the floor
still alive
and then she was lying on that bench
and she was dead.

It was nothing but a piece of fur.

Even with an animal
it's quite obvious
when the soul has departed.

That's not something you take home.

And where would I bury her?

Peter had a book by a . . .
a woman who won a Nobel prize . . .
he gave it to me, it's up there.

Yesterday they were saying on the radio
that this woman
had collected the stories
of the last people still alive
who'd been children during the war.

All of those who'd been children then.

When I heard that yesterday
my thought was I shan't read it.

I thought it was all so boring
after all, I'd been there myself.

The house in Hagen was built
by my grandfather's ancestors.

He was born in eighteen seventy-four.

Grandma was born in eighteen ninety-one
so she was seventeen years younger.

Which made a really big age difference between them.

I said to her once
Why did you take such an old man?

She said
Ah, but he was handsome, was Hagen's Per.

Dad said
they were staying out at the Osebol shieling
when the war was raging in Norway
and they could hear the guns.

There were lots of service people who came here at that time.

A man who'd been stationed here came back
he was from Arboga.

He stayed at the campsite
along with his wife.

I saw them coming
and said to Dad
Any idea who they are?

The man came in
but she stayed outside
so I went out.

Well, he said,
I used to live here
during the war.

And how did he put it . . .
The shack hasn't changed at all, he said.

He recognised the cottage.

It was exactly the same
as it was when they came here.

I said
Come away in.

I was baking buns
and had a full pastry board.

I made coffee
and they sat there chatting.

He talked about how they
would carry hay into the bedroom
and sleep on the floor.

I had a farm back then, he said
So when midsummer came
I was allowed to return home.

Nanny at Halvarsgårn . . .
she never had a family.

She was like a man, know what I mean?
more like a man.

You should have seen her
when she came marching along.

Some sight I can tell you!

She was very mannish.

Of course, it may well be
that she was that way inclined.

I just don't know.

She never got married
and as far as anyone knew
never had a boyfriend.

But she really was a kind-hearted soul.

They didn't have a telephone at Halvarsgårn
but we had one here.

Anyone who wanted to get hold of them
would ring us
and we had to go over with the message.

Every Christmas
I got a Christmas present from her
for running so many errands.

She was the best sort, she really was.

I can picture her now.

I remember how she'd answer the phone
when their phone number was still five four
before we got these long numbers.

When you phoned there she'd say
Five fourrr!

Five fourrr!

I don't know where she got that rrr from.

Mum and Dad were divorced.

I didn't have a mother really.

She'd left.

So it was Dad's sisters, Karin and Lilly
and Grandma
that I grew up with . . .
and Dad too.

But I don't think I suffered . . .
I had a good childhood
with things the way they were.

She lived in Malung.

She was a leather seamstress there.

There was a teacher in Stöllet.

He took Years Five, Six, Seven at the school.

He was the District Head Teacher
and it was written on everything he owned.

On his rulers and everything else.

District Head Teacher.

God help us, a fellow like that.

I'll never forget the time . . .
Leif who lived here
just north of the bridge
with his mum
because he didn't have a dad.

Once when we were in a lesson.

Leif hadn't put his hand up
but was made to answer anyway.

He didn't know the answer
and the teacher said
Well, I wouldn't expect any better
after all, he hasn't got a father
he said
in front of all the children.

I was in Year Five then
and he was in Six.

He said that
and I thought it was awful.

Perhaps it got to me
because I didn't have a mother.

That's probably it.

Because I didn't have a mother around.

That's why I sort of really felt it.

I think of all the people
I've seen on T V
who go abroad
to find out about their parents.

My mother lived in Malung
and never got in touch.

I would catch sight of her every now and again
when I was in Malung
in the shops and the like.

I got a silver bracelet
for my confirmation.

Never anything else.

I've never known
anyone
apart from Grandma
and Karin and Lilly
and Dad.

But life has been good to me.

We went on to the continuation school
in Ruskåsen
and cut timber.

For twelve weeks.

God, that long!

We slept at the school in Ruskåsen.

That was when we were fourteen.

They called it continuation school
which meant the school kitchen.

They sent us out to the forest instead.

But in those days the boys
learned to bake and cook.

Really? Did they now?

Yes, they did!

They used to throw dough at each other and . . .

It was OK
but cutting timber was hard work
as young as that.

When I left school I became a timber measurer.

That involves holding a chain, two of you
and measuring logs.

They were known as dogs on chains!

One person measured the width with callipers
and someone else made a note of it.

This was down along the river.

Trees were being measured up for logging firms.

We used a little axe
to cut a mark
in the end of the log.

That showed
it had already been measured.

We were living in the forestry lodge
at Granberget at that time.

How old was I?

Fourteen, fifteen, sixteen.

We were paid eighteen crowns a day.

Cheap.

Cheap labour.

But it was a long time ago.

Hans Emilsson 1939–2019
Ingalill Hagström 1942–2021 | 155

In nineteen sixty-three
I joined the Klarälv Timber Rafting Co-op
and worked for them for ten years.

Timber was being floated down the river here.

The companies employed the raftsmen.

Uddeholm and Billerud and Vargön
and the rest.

I spent the winters at home in Ändenäs
hauling out logs with a horse.

I frequently worked the boat from Deje
taking timber through the locks
in Forshaga.

One time the logs had to be taken
all the way to Skoghall.

Gösta . . .
his name was Gösta Larsson as I remember . . .
asked me
What the hell are we going to do
when we get to Karlstad?

Well, I said
You'll have to drive so slowly
that the boat is hardly moving.

On the bend in the river by the Stadshotellet
there used to be a café on a boat
where you could get coffee in the summer.

A bloody big boat.

But Gösta Larsson
went at top speed.

He went so fast
that his load
swept right into the floating café.

It cost the Klarälv Timber Rafting Co-op
thirty-seven thousand crowns
to get the shambles fixed.

Most of the time I was up in the sorting area.

Sorting out pine and spruce.

Pine with pine, spruce with spruce.

                              Didn't a man come floating once, on the river?

Yes, a man came down.

He went into the river in Munkfors on Christmas Eve.

His footsteps were found in the snow.

He came down to Deje with the logs.

Hjalmar, he came from Skoga,
said
I've worked at Lake Lusten by Deje
for twenty-seven years
and along comes this one
and I've no idea
what the hell kind it is.

Then men came up
from Karlstad.

They had gloves
that went right up to here.

And the minister from Deje came.

It should be like that every day
Hjalmar said.

The chipboard factory was looking for people
in seventy-two.

So I got to start there
in the steam section.

We were there
several days and nights
waiting for the first sheet
to come.

And it was never ready.

But eventually one night it was
and bugger me it was good.

It was so hush-hush
and they chopped
that sheet into pieces.

We were all there
all of us who were on that shift.

What was his name now . . . Wennerström . . .
he was the one responsible
for people turning up
being where they were supposed to be.

He'd come and say
You be here tomorrow?
then he'd take off his hat.

You never had time to say yes
or anything else.

Good, he'd say
and walk off.

Later I worked in the chipping section.

My job was to look after the machines
producing wood chips.

The pulpwood came in through the wall
on a conveyor belt
and passed through a chipper
that chopped it up.

There were weighing machines
that weighed it in.

Two machines would mix the glue
in the glue shop.

From there it passed on
to the forming machine.

Which moved backwards slowly, slowly, slowly
laying down a layer of chips . . .
maybe
some ten, fifteen centimetres thick.

From there it went on to the press.

That made it twenty-two millimetres
or twelve millimetres
or ten millimetres.

All depending on how they wanted the board to be.

It's all been sold up now.

God, what a mess they made of the factory.

They just knocked holes through the walls
and pulled out everything
it was all to be taken away.

Terrible . . .
the number of people they let go.

                                        More than forty.

                        If you look at it in proportion . . .
                                Stockholm and here.

                                It was a terrible blow.

Come the end, they were producing chips
here in Norra Ny
and taking them by lorry
to Lit in Östersund
and selling them there.

As the fellows from Lit said
It would be a damn sight better
for the lorries to pick them up here
and take them where they were supposed to go
rather than load them here
take them to Östersund
unload them
and then reload them
to take them where they were supposed to go.

I served as churchwarden
last Epiphany.

My function is
to robe the minister.

And usually then
I'll hand out the hymn books . . .
stand down by the door
and hand them out.

Then take the collection.

More people attend
when there's a special event of some kind
but apart from that
on an ordinary Sunday
there won't be very many
maybe a dozen or so.

Once, when I served as churchwarden
that's a few years ago
after Birgitta Halvarsson became our minister.

She was living in Karlstad at the time
and I was the churchwarden on the Sunday
when not a single person turned up.

I said to her
Did you come all the way from Karlstad
to take the service?

Yes, she said
but I'm going on to Dalby too
to take the service there.

No one came.

She read a lesson from the Bible
and we sang a hymn
and we just went home.

But there's only been the one occasion
when a service wasn't held.

He makes coffee for me
so I get it when I come down in the morning.

                              Yes, she hasn't done it for five years.

Then Stig Över comes
at half past six in the morning
and stays a couple of hours.

Then Birgit comes.

Time passes so slowly she says
I just have to get out.

Ingalill Hagström 1942–2021
Hans Emilsson 1939–2019 | *169*

Half past four yesterday afternoon Hans said
I don't suppose anyone else will come today
I'll lock up
but we didn't lock the door
and all of a sudden two people arrived.

It was Birgit and Stig.

She'd been out walking with poles
and was right outside our house
and then there was Stig driving down
so they got here at the same time.

When they get here Birgit says
Here comes the night shift.

The chaffinches have arrived back now.

Isn't that a chaffinch, on the ground over there?

With red on its . . .

                                        No . . . o.

It is, it's a chaffinch.

Ingalill Hagström 1942–2021
Hans Emilsson 1939–2019 | *171*

I came here in the autumn of nineteen forty
when I was a year old
I've lived here ever since.

I was with Granny and Grandpa most of the time
because Mum and Dad
were busy in the shop.

It was so cold and they said
this lass will die of cold.

It's called Källdalen
it was really boggy
and poor for firewood.

The man who built the shop
was called Helmer Carlsson
that was sometime in thirty-seven, thirty-eight
but then it went bust.

We came in nineteen forty.

So it was a case of starting from scratch again.

There were quite a few people
in every cottage
and no cars.

Out at Storberg there was a communal kitchen . . .
forestry workers could live there
during the week.

There was another one at Granberg
that they drove supplies out to.

They had barracks there
and a woman to cook the food
so they could go there to eat.

They had horses and everything.

There was a Konsum Co-op in Stöllet
farther north than where it is now
and there was Grahn's
across the river here
and two shops in Värnäs
and one at Lindmon
and two in Ambjörby and in Månäs
that's how many there were.

And there was one in Torp
and two in Fastnäs
both a Konsum Co-op and a private shop
and in Gravol there were two.

That many
and there were enough people to keep all that going.

People often kept a pig and a cow
and a calf and chickens
but they still had shopping to do.

Dad was called up.

He was in western Värmland
Mum managed as best she could
together with David from Sandvik
who was Annie and Daniel's son
he helped out
and there was someone from Stöllet
who helped out too.

Dad was away
I don't know how long for
so it really wasn't easy.

There were ration cards
for everything
and they had to be clipped
and sent in.

I just don't know how Mum
managed all that.

During the winter
we spent a lot of time at Ävjan
south of Armgard's.

There was much more snow in those days.

We had an ice-skating track there.

During the summer we often went swimming
down by the meadow here
and down in Fiskenäs.

The water level used to be more stable all the time
but after the river regulation scheme
it became really unpredictable.

They used to float logs down the river.

And afterwards they'd go along cleaning up.

The last logs were known as
the arse end.

I was involved in measuring length.

I used to measure the logs
together with another person.

It was horrendously cold.

There were great stacks of logs just south of here
where the timber trucks unloaded them
and then they would be measured
before being put into the river.

But this was all a long, long time ago.

We used skis all the time
Mum and Dad
Christer and me.

We had ski trails in the fields and
there was a thing called the Snow Star badge
that Arne at Byggninga and I
and a couple of others
around here had.

You had to ski so-and-so many times
and you were given a stitch-on badge.

Those were the winter activities around here.

We weren't spoilt
by being taken everywhere by car.

When we used to visit Granny and Grandpa
in Sunne, or Torsberg
we had snow up here
but when we got there
there was hardly ever any snow.

We had gigantic snowdrifts here
Daniel at Sandvik had a horse
and a thing
like a great big scoop
that he used to shovel up the snow
he piled it up by the roadside at Halvarsgårn
where it got really hard-packed.

He cleared the snow here in Osebol
cleared it at Hemgårn and at our place.

People think that almost every house
has its own tractor.

In those days they didn't
but they'd have a horse.

School went up to Year Seven
and after that
it was on to the Hermods Vocational School in Stöllet
and a continuation course in Ljusnästorp.

Stöllet wasn't the only school
there was one in Ennarbol too, which they call Back
and one in Ljusnästorp.

There must have been plenty of children.

I went to the Hermods for a bit
you were supposed to go on down to Malmö
but I didn't complete it.

When I came home I went into the shop
and stayed to the end more or less.

From fifty-five
and then, after that . . .
well, time just rolled by.

Mum passed away two thousand and eight.

That's when we shut the shop, before Christmas
and in two thousand and nine we sold up.

Mum and Dad were there the whole time.

Dad passed away two thousand and five.

As long as they were alive things just carried on.

For seventy years near enough.

It's been a way of life.

Every day more or less the same.

When I was smaller . . .
since Mum and Dad were in the shop
if anyone had maybe
forgotten something
all they had to do was pop in.

Christmas Eve . . . the shop used to be open.

When Christina was born I said
now we're going to celebrate Christmas Eve
like everyone else
and not open the shop.

But this was sort of met with resistance.

You mean we should close on Christmas Eve?

Yes, close on Christmas Eve
and that's what happened.

We had shop assistants
one from Sunne and others too
so Mum and Dad
weren't all alone.

In the nineteen seventies they started going abroad.

Otherwise we went to Dalarna a lot
that was a sort of tradition.

The round of Lake Siljan
and something called the TT race in Hedemora
a motor-bike race.

Dalarna was really beautiful.

We'd go on a Sunday
since the shop was closed then
and we could get away for the day.

Ingalill and I
lived across the road from one another.

I lived in the shop
and she lived down there.

Tage and Hans lived in Ändenäs.

They went to school in Ljusnästorp
but it wasn't far away anyway.

I was the one who met Tage first.

We got engaged in sixty-one
and got married in sixty-five.

Last November would have been our fiftieth anniversary.

He went to the vocational school in Säffle.

That's why we were there for a while.

And he became a carpenter.

They'd built
this log house
in Ändenäs.

That's where you're sitting now.

At that stage we thought we'd maybe have it
as a summer cottage.

We didn't know
if we'd be living in Säffle.

Then we thought
Well, perhaps we could build something here.

Stöllet was suggested first of all
but we didn't want that.

The houses are so close to each other there.

No open space.

We wanted to live in a place on its own
not that 'compact living' as they call it.

We wanted a house that was on its own
but still close.

So we enquired with Holmen farm down here
with Vilhelm as the owner then was called
and he said there wouldn't be a problem.

It was completely empty here
lots of trees in front
so couldn't be overlooked at all.

That's why we built here.

When we had the shop . . .
big boxes of cold meats would arrive.

Butcher meat and everything.

You could send in an order
and it would come to Torsby
and then come on the bus
dropped off at the door.

And then all the deliveries in ICA vans.

But it's really strange
the way things have developed.

Most of the stuff is semi-processed these days.

ICA Groceries became really huge.

They decided
that now you had to buy
ten boxes, say, of an item
when you used to be able to buy
just one box.

They were bossing you around.

Lots of people gave up.

I carried on
until eventually I thought it's time to stop.

Everything had to be computerised
everything cost money
terminals and card readers
it all got so expensive.

I didn't have rent to pay
so I could hang on a bit longer.

But they're killing off the little people.

Who are just supposed to find some way of surviving.

Oh, what a lovely area and beautiful . . . bla, bla.

But you can't live on air, can you?

We organised provisions
for the river rafters.

Things were going really well in the last years.

Enough to keep us going.

Wilderness Värmland would order goods
which we'd make up
for three-day tours or week-long tours
and they'd come and collect them.

They had places at Osebol Meadow
as well as Ytnäs Meadow.

But there were plenty of people on the river
who came to visit
without being organised by them.

We had a sign by the bridge
and another down by the river meadow.

We did everything from coffee and tea
to butter and bread
and cheese and meat and fish
and cornflakes and bread.

They only had cool bags
and ice packs . . .
we used to change their packs for them.

Canned food was what they wanted
not so much fresh food.

And they'd perhaps be going fishing.

There are supposed to be grayling in the river
and possibly perch and some pike
not that I'd know.

Can you see me with a fishing rod?

I'll sit in the sun and enjoy it
but I'd never sit down with a fishing rod
no chance of that.

Then we had a big project
with Stödalen.

We put a good few hours into that.

How to set about
creating a slalom course . . .
I'm pretty sure it was Alvar's idea.

We sold membership cards for five kronor
and believe it or not everyone bought one.

The hillside had to be cleared
and we brought in machinery
to do it.

Everyone gave their time unpaid.

The whole time.

But when volunteering ended
everything else came to an end too.

That's what happened.

Lars and Christina would come home from school . . .
Look, the lights on the slope are on
let's go.

That really was something
managing to get a ski lift
and a hut and everything.

Tage and Alvar went to Kil
and bought the hut.

Later we even had a lighted ski trail.

It was unbelievable
but now it's . . .
the poles are down
and there's nothing.

I don't know whether young people
have got more demanding
and maybe the slope was too small.

Because then came Branäs
and there was Hovfjället.

We used to go to Hovfjället with the children
when the weather was good
but later we tended to stay here.

The slope was open three nights a week
and there were people there all the time.

We had a plan
and it worked.

No one had any complaints.

It was the highways agency
and then the local authority.

It became impossible to get anywhere.

Then came the final nail in the coffin.

Costs, of course
and the traffic
at the east end of the bridge . . .
it's quite narrow there.

We carried on as long as we could
but eventually ran out of energy.

That's what happened.

But at least we still have a fine bridge.

It's still there, anyway.

Farther up the valley
in Sysslebäck
is where it's all happening
and we'll be left as a dot on the map.

There won't be much going on here.

They're investing more up there
than down here in Stöllet.

It's the council
and you can't say so out loud
but you can think it, can't you?

We used to be very involved
with the Nysocken market.

We used to hold it down in the field
at Halvarsgårn.

It was much more welcoming
than at Ytnäs Meadow where it is now.

The old-fashioned market feel
has been lost.

It must have been very nearly ten years.

There was a theatre group and everything you can think of.

There were preparations to be done in advance
tents to be put up
refreshments organised.

We were young in those days and everyone helped out.

Loads of people . . .
like the people at Bråten
and those at Hagen who . . .
they all said
We'll bake, we'll donate!

Everyone joined in the whole time
got involved
and we made money.

When we ran the Easter auction
the school hall was so full people were out in the corridor.

That's how involved people got.

There was so much community spirit.

These days people don't know
the meaning of volunteering . . .
they expect to be paid for their time.

And that's the end of community spirit.

That's what's so sad.

Some people say
the trend will change.

Well, when do you think that's going to happen?

We've got any number of cottages
standing empty here.

They buy a house here
the Dutch, for instance
for a couple of hundred thousand
and maybe sell their place
down there for millions.

Then they move here
intending to make a living out of tourism
but not everyone can make a living that way.

Nowadays people can work
from wherever they happen to be
but as I say
they have to have something to live on.

They can't just sell their house
and live on the money forever.

We've got empty sites
there's the chipboard factory
up at Krusmon
which could offer great opportunities.

But apart from all the forests
what else have we got to offer?

I go over to Karin's a lot.

She and I have a lot in common.

We support each other.

Karin phoned
just as I came in yesterday.

She'd already phoned earlier in the day.

She knew I was away
but wanted to check
that I'd got home.

Ingalill phoned too.

She'd been trying to get me on my mobile
but it was in the pocket of my jacket
and I hadn't noticed
it ringing.

Both Karin and Ingalill phone
to check whether I'm here.

But I've left a key at Hagen.

That's what I've done.

That's the way of it.

We have a sewing circle
but we don't do much sewing.

It's a social activity
and that's important, isn't it?

Once a week
or sometimes it might be a fortnight
all depending.

When Mum was alive
she always started on the seventh of January
that was her birthday
and that's when the meetings started.

I've tried to stick to
the tradition
but it was so dreadfully cold this year
that I only went to her grave.

When we were in Stödalen
we took it in turns for a while
but we changed that
when Karin was ill.

I said to her
Karin, do you want us to come to you?

That would mean we'll still be able to meet.

And she wouldn't be left out.

We have to try
to keep it going.

Now we're over at Karin's
and every other time here at my place.

We make coffee
and each of us brings her own food.

There's to be no special cleaning
just take us as you find us.

It was Annie Ekberg and Mum who started it.

Mum would've been a hundred and one now
and Annie Ekberg was older.

It must have been seventy years ago.

We put in twenty crowns each time
enough for an Easter meal and Christmas dinner.

We used to be able to go somewhere
but now we're older
some of us can't manage the travel.

But we'll go and have a meal in Ambjörby
once everything's finished there.

It's going to be a café.

We organize it as a sort of study circle
through the WEA and the pensioners' organisation
and I hold the papers.

We have boules too.

It's at the pool by Hotel Gästis.

We began by playing at the ice-hockey rink
when it was closed down.

Then we used the football pitch.

When they filled in the swimming pool
the council made boules pitches for us.

They've made a meeting room
in the building
where people used to change for swimming lessons.

We've had the odd meeting there.

We might hold a special evening.

We invited people to that once or twice
because we had the money.

Then we held it in there.

I was amazed that Mum
wanted to buy this house.

Most of it was in a bloody awful state.

Mould and rotten tubs everywhere.

I was really disappointed
the first time I came here.

I thought it was beautiful
with the river and the bridge
but the house
was hellish.

Birds had got in.

Some of the windows were broken
and they just flew in.

She said
Just you wait and see.

It's going to be a dream house.

We were lucky with that winter.

While we were building the foundations and chimney stack
it was twelve degrees
in the middle of December.

Sunny, too.

Otherwise it would have taken us much longer.

I went to a boarding school
and stayed here when I was home in the holidays.

After high school
I went on to Örebro to study.

When I finished my course
I was about to start on the next one . . .
another three or four years.

But Dad passed away.

I decided
to stop studying
and come home
to help Mum.

When Dad passed away
the minister came
to talk about him
and the kind of funeral we wanted.

The minister told us
this used to be a mission house
but I can see you've turned it
into a house to be lived in.

She wasn't the only one to say that,
others said the same thing.

Said it was good that
somebody had converted a building
that was falling apart
into a house that's a kind of visiting card
for the district.

We are Poles.

We're more open
than anything we've seen
here in Sweden.

There's a difference
when it comes to human contact
and celebrations.

If you want to get together
in Poland
you just knock on your neighbour's door
and go in.

It's not like that here.

At least, it doesn't feel like it.

It feels as if you have to book a time
before you can meet anyone.

They're uptight . . .
though they do open up, the Swedes do
when they've got a drink in them.

That's what I mean with the celebrations.

They came as a shock to me.

When you go to a party
you probably won't get any food
as you would in Poland
nor any alcohol
as you would in Poland.

I suppose it's because alcohol
is so expensive
and difficult to get hold of too.

Everyone brings
their own bottles
and they're already fed and drunk when they arrive
and they don't usually share
what they've brought with them.

When I invite people to a party
they often ask
Is it really OK to help myself?

Are you sure?

Of course I'm sure
I wouldn't have offered otherwise.

The attitudes I've come across in Osebol
aren't like that.

It's more like Poland.

You can knock on someone's door
without having arranged to meet.

Just drop in for coffee
biscuits
or a beer.

In Poland
we lived in a city the size of Stockholm
Łódź.

When we moved here
I thought the place was dead
but now I can't imagine
living in a city.

When I visit friends
in Stockholm or Örebro
or Karlstad
I end up feeling exhausted after a couple of hours.

When we go to Poland
it's just the same.

I don't have the energy for anything.

The traffic chaos
and the poor air
give me a headache.

When I'm talking to Swedes
I Swedicise the name.

When they see Ł – ó – d – ź
they say Lodz.

It's pronounced Wodz
but if I say Wodz
they just go Wo . . . Wo . . . ?

That's why I've changed my name
from Maciej to Mattias
when I'm in Sweden.

It makes it easier
for Swedes to pronounce.

Instead of them standing there
for five minutes going
Masj . . . what did you say?

Mum and I have both changed our names.

It's worked.

We've kept exactly the same names
but the Swedish equivalents.

There's a film
I'd like to recommend.
It's called Seksmisja in Polish.

In translation that means something like
'sex mission'.

It's about a world
in which an atom bomb
kills men, only men.

Just two men are left
and they are deep-frozen.

They wake and see
there are only women
in the whole world.

It's an entertaining film.

Everyone I show it to laughs
because it's actually quite topical
in view of
the way society is developing in Sweden.

What with feminism
and everything having to be equal.

In my view, men are losing out
in this equality business.

Maybe you don't agree with me
but I think what usually happens is
that things are equal
as long as women win.

Take studying at university.

It shouldn't be easier for women
to gain a doctorate, for instance.

It should be the same.

Where's everything going to end up
if it's made easier for women?

Women won't get jobs.

People will think
OK, it was easier for you
so you're probably not so smart
as the men.

It shouldn't be easier
for one sex or the other
to get something.

I get called a sexist.

No, you mustn't say things like that
we must have equality.

We have plenty of equality
but it shouldn't be made easier for you
to get a job
or easier to get a chance to study.

In my view we shouldn't be judging
on whether it's a man or a woman.

We should judge
on whether it's a good job
or a bad job.

That's how I'd like it to be.

Just like that.

It's not just about women and men
it's also about being foreign
or not foreign.

That can often be an issue too.

Being foreign
can make things easier
because no one wants
to be called a racist.

I've actually played that card myself
when I've got really annoyed
with someone in the shop.

It always works.

But I don't think
it should be used.

Whether someone is black, red, yellow or green
has nothing to do with it.

If you do a good job
you do a good job.

Poles have always seen the West
as superior to them
as somewhere to be looked up to.

They want to reach the same level that
Germany, France
USA, England or Sweden
used to have.

I think that in
twenty, thirty, fifty years
things will change.

Germans
will come to work in Poland
instead of Poles
moving to Germany to work.

One day we'll wake up
and notice
Aha, we're the superior ones now.

Many businesses
are moving their headquarters or their factories
to Poland.

Taxes are lower
the workforce is cheaper
materials are cheaper
virtually everything is cheaper.

And people also work better.

The average German worker
comes to work at eight.

Has a break at half past nine
lunch at eleven
there's another break at half past twelve
and so on with break, break, break
all the time.

When a Pole is working
he arrives at eight and finishes at six.

No breaks.

The break can come afterwards.

I worked on a farm
one summer.

My job was to unscrew the metal sheets
on a big tractor shed
so wooden planks could be fitted instead.

They'd estimated
it would take me a week to do it.

I said
A week for this?

It took one day.

They just . . .
How the hell did you do that?

I didn't take a coffee break
fag break
pee break
lunch break
break break
I just worked.

Why not just get on
and get things finished one by one
instead of working a little while
and then taking a break?

You either work hard
or not at all
nothing in between.

That's not something
I've learnt from
the Swedes.

When I came to Sweden
health care was much better here.

Dentists
everything to do with medicine.

Now I'd say
it's better in Poland.

It's cheaper to go to the airport
take a flight to Poland
get my teeth fixed
and return here
than to go to Torsby or Malung
to get my teeth done.

And the waiting times . . .

Some time ago Mum broke her arm.

She went to the hospital
and they said
You'll have to wait two months
for an X-ray.

We took a direct flight
and had an X-ray done in ten minutes.

Many things in Sweden are getting worse
but when I say it to Swedes
they answer
No, no, no
everything is good
everything is fine, just right.

I've lived in a city.

Studied in Örebro.

It's not for me.

I'd rather live here.

But it's a pity there aren't
very many young people here.

I think Värmland as a whole would benefit
if people were allowed to build houses
right by the river
like ours is.

It would give some encouragement
to anyone thinking of moving away.

Living by the water
is really great
but you don't usually get to do it.

It's either extremely expensive
or you're not allowed to build there.

It's wonderful in the summer
except for all the mosquitoes.

We usually light a bonfire
and that gets rid of them a bit.

We burn the weeds
to make more smoke.

Sprays and creams
none of them work.

We bought a machine
but that didn't work either.

Mosquitoes
or tiny little midges
or deer flies.

They are a sort of cross
between spiders and mosquitoes and flies.

Hellish creatures.

There can be a bit of a problem
at the end of winter.

In April, May
when the river rises.

We worry
there'll be a landslip
and the house will collapse into the water.

Occasionally in summer
when it's hot
the river almost disappears.

You can't do any fishing
or take a trip in the boat.

You'd just get stuck on a sandbank.

It's because of the power station at Höljes.

The river rises and falls
instead of staying
at the same level.

They've talked about
removing the bridge.

I think it would be a pity.

They offered to sell it to us
for one krona
but we said no.

We'd have to renovate it
every year
and see to the upkeep
and we didn't want that.

It's fine the way it is.

When the weather's hot in the summer
you can run or cycle
doing the round of the bridges.

It's a fair distance to cover.

It's a pity, though,
that there's no footway
on the other side.

And it's very narrow.

You don't show up too well
even wearing a Hi-Viz vest.

It doesn't matter on this side.

There's not so much traffic
over here.

It's just when you're doing
the circuit of the bridges.

Back home in Bohuslän
almost everyone
was forced to emigrate to America.

Some of them did well
and some of them came home
as poor
as when they set out.

My father went.

Three of his brothers also went.

He returned home.

Destitute.

Two of the brothers did well.

They came home
after making quite a lot of money.

There was a huge difference between them.

He worked in the coal mines.

He stayed there five years.

He didn't earn enough for a ticket home
and Mum had to send him enough for the journey.

That's what happened.

I remember
German planes on their way to Norway.

They were flying so low
you could see the crew.

The treetops swayed as they flew over.

It was terrifying.

There were huge naval battles off the coast.

Even though it was a long way away
you could see flames and things
in the evenings and at night.

Worst of all were the planes flying over
swarms of them.

You could see the men
sitting in the plane.

I had to help Mum
until I was called up
and then I disappeared too.

My brother who was a bit older than me
became a seaman.

He died at sea.

He died down in Rotterdam.

Fell headlong
into the empty hold of the ship.

They were covering it with a tarpaulin
when he plummeted down into the cargo hold.

He was twenty-one.

Accidents have always happened
and always will happen.

It was a really decent shipping company
and they wanted to pay Mum compensation.

But she turned it down.

Me getting money
she said
is not going to bring him back.

And I think she was right.

My partner came from up here
and wanted to come back.

She came from a place called Baskenäsmon
up above Ambjörby.

Her roots were up here
so it's not surprising.

We used to rent a cabin every summer
at Värnäs Campsite.

We'd been out picking berries
and we came across signs for houses for sale.

So that settled it.

When you move up here . . .
well, it's not like down there.

If you went to the shop
to buy a loaf
you expected it to be freshly baked
and preferably still warm.

But when things aren't in stock
you have to wait days
maybe weeks.

You wouldn't accept that down there . . .
you'd just think
Shut this place down.

You took everything for granted.

You were really demanding
but it's no good being like that here.

Since then I've got to see
a lot more.

People who are crippled
and wracked with pain
but good and happy in spite of it.

You never noticed that sort of thing
down there.

There was the job and nothing but the job . . .

It's all very different now.

I was thinking today about . . .
Biskopsgården.

When I started work
in the factory producing prefabs
there wasn't a single house there.

That was nineteen fifty-nine.

It was all forest like round here.

The company bought the forest
and felled it.

I hauled the timber.

You simply couldn't imagine
it was going to become
the kind of housing development
it became.

All you could see then
were stumps and stones.

If only the people living there
knew what it used to look like.

Landvetter Airport
was just the same.

Nothing but forest and rocks
there too.

Nobody could have imagined
there would be an airport there.

Wow, that took some blasting.

There were awkward outcrops of rock.

And bogs.

And the land round the airport
provided world-class berry picking.

That's all gone, of course.

I go to church occasionally
on Christmas Day and the like.

I've sat there full of admiration . . .
just studying the planks in the walls.

Thinking of the men
who cut down the trees
and the horses that hauled them
to where they were to be split.

If you went to a woodyard now
and tried to buy planks like that
they'd have a heart attack.

I've lost a truly wonderful neighbour.

Bo Nilsson.

He used to call me stock manager.

He needed a lot of help
down there in the garage.

When he was out on the road
or in the forest
something would always break
and he'd phone me.

Go down and get the van
and bring this and that with you.

He had one of those Mercedes breakdown vans.

Life will be empty.

He would always turn out.

However late it was.

If someone
needed help on Christmas Eve
he would turn out.

There was that road grader of his.

In winter it was used for snow ploughing
and spring, summer and autumn
it was used for improving the roads.

He drove timber transports
and he also had a job clearing snow
over in Fensbol.

He phoned at four o'clock in the morning,

I knew it must be an emergency call-out.

Bror, I forgot to bring my lunch box.

Can you bring my wallet too?

It's in the knife drawer.

OK, but what if Marianne wakes up?

You'll just have to deal with it, he said.

He needed fuel
and his fuel card was in his wallet.

I had to go in through the garage
as the front door was locked.

Luckily she didn't wake up
because I had no idea how I'd explain
why I was standing there rummaging in their knife drawer.

On the other hand
she was probably used to most things.

But it was really good
for me too.

Made me feel I was still of some use.

And he was one of the old school
which meant that he and I had been through
more or less the same things.

That's what made it so easy
to get on with him.

I used to spend Christmas Eve down at their place
after I was on my own here.

He came up here and said to me
Come on down this evening
and have Christmas dinner with us.

I couldn't manage it last Christmas
because I was bent double.

I was in dreadful pain.

And had the shivers.

I just sat by the stove.

The cats just sat there looking at me
wondering what was the matter.

I was shaking like an aspen leaf.

He came up on Christmas morning
to see how things were going.

There was no change.

I was still bent double.

Time to get dressed he said
it's the A&E for you.

When I got there two nurses
took charge of me.

One of them asked
Why didn't you come in sooner with this?

You know as well as I do, the other one said
what grumpy, difficult old men are like.

In spite of all the pain I was in
I couldn't help laughing
at how right she was.

We'd spent
the day before he died
adjusting and fixing the grader.

During the afternoon . . .
Well, he said
that'll be enough for today.

So we went off our separate ways as usual
intending
to come back to the job the following day.

I took a look down there
and couldn't see the blue van
which made me think
he's probably taking a day off today.

Now I just potter about to help the time pass.

When he was alive
there was always something for me to go and fetch.

I used to go and collect spare parts
or go and pick him up.

Let's put it like this . . .
he was the only one
I had anything to do with up here.

I think he could have been given
a few more years.

It was at a dance at Ambjörby community centre.

I like dancing.

Åke was there and I knew
he was a very good dancer.

We danced a bit in the course of the evening
and in a funny way
I had strong feelings for Åke.

Something
clicked in my head
that he was the one for me.

He was already taken.

But I went up to him
and said
Åke, will you have the last dance with me?
and so he danced with me.

There was nothing definite just then
but I felt
there was something between us.

Åke's mum was living here then.

She thought the place was too big
and living here was too much work
so she looked for a flat in Stöllet.

That's when we took it over.

It was hard-going in the beginning.

I felt very lonely
because Åke was working
as much as he did
at Gammelbyn holiday village.

I talked to him about it
and he understood.

I'm getting on really well now
I really am.

I'm not the sort of person
that surrounds themself with friends.

I can be sociable
but I don't actually need mates.

I'm like that, I don't know why.

But I felt there were so few people here.

Probably because I'd lived in a flat
and we'd socialised in that way.

We could have a game of cards.

We had people up close.

When I came here and it was empty
I thought it was awful.

I didn't know anyone at all.

And I thought . . . is this where I'm going to live?

I trained as an assistant nurse.

There was something called validation
and those of us who'd worked in the health system
had a chance . . .

I applied and got in.

Since it was validation
there wasn't an exam.

We had to study and do group presentations.

I found it horrendously difficult
to begin with
but a teacher managed to convince me
to complete the course.

I'm qualified
for everything I've done
and that feels good.

I have a sense of freedom in going out
visiting old people in their homes.

They tell me about their lives
and I can sit and listen.

I feel that
what I'm doing fulfils a purpose.

Care improved
after grouping was brought in.

Before that they had to go round and attend to everyone
and bedsores were common.

But eventually you hardly saw any at all.

Partly because anyone who could be got out of bed was got up.

We had more time.

And dressings and bandages and that kind of thing improved too.

Mattresses became much better.

It wasn't just the grouping as such
but also the great developments
in nursing and health care.

You seldom see anyone
with pressure sores these days.

I think that's really wonderful.

I'd been working in long-term care for twelve years
and felt I had no more to give.

They were advertising for a kitchen assistant
in the kitchen in Likenäs.

I applied and got the job.

Those of us who'd worked a certain length of time
in kitchens in the Torsby district
got to go on a course
at Nygård domestic school in Ekshärad.

We did cooking and baking there.

The theory was sometimes done in Stöllet
at Klarastrand old people's home.

People came there from Höljes
and Torsby and Östmark.

For those with a long way to come
Stöllet was a halfway point.

And it showed we have something to offer here too.

I worked in the kitchen for seven years.

We cooked all the meals from scratch.

Breakfast, lunch, evening meal.

At Christmas we cooked Christmas dinner from scratch.

Christmas sausage, home-baked bread
cardamom bread, sponge cake.

I think long-term care
should have been kept.

It was good
for people who didn't have any relatives.

And the catering kitchen
should have been kept.

The food they get now
is all semi-processed.

They asked me
whether I would consider
going out as a home help.

I felt very negative about it
since I had a fixed workplace.

Going into homes and people's private things
and their money . . .
I was reluctant about that.

Going into other people's houses
must feel strange, I thought.

But then I said to myself
I can't just say no
without giving it a try anyway.

And that's what I did
and enjoyed it more than I can say.

Things have changed.

Everything has to be given approval these days.

If you have a client
who wants cleaning done
or wants to be taken for a walk
or given a shower
you must get approval.

You have to apply
to the care manager for Torsby district.
to get it.

Then they work out roughly
the length of time you will have to spend there.

You will maybe need about half an hour
for a shower.

It's not all about exact timing . . .
just so you have something to go on.

We're not allowed to do anything
unless it has been given approval.

There are some days when
I might drive as much as sixty miles.

And it's not unknown
for us to be unable to reach
the client
without having to walk some of the way.

It might be snow
maybe ice even.

We're usually on our own in the car.

It's rare for there to be two of us.

I have the radio sometimes.

I've also learnt to unwind
while driving the car.

I relax and gather my thoughts
while driving to the next place.

I've got better at doing it.

The job I'd really like to be doing
is chiropody.

I've always liked it.

I used to do it sometimes
when I was working in long-term care.

Some people think
the business of cutting nails and so on
is absolutely disgusting . . . oh well . . .

Some of the people who came to me
just couldn't deal with the nails
on their hands and feet.

But I really felt good, oh, I really did
when I had the chance to do it.

I remember one client
who had real problems.

I said
If you'll just put your feet in the footbath
I'll look after you.

He trusted me
and I knew this was something I could do.

I can deal with this.

And I did.

I'd have liked to be able to drive to their homes.

Chiropody on wheels.

But at the time I was thinking about it
it wasn't here
it was too far distant
and I had young children
so it was one of those thoughts
I had to put out of my head
though in other circumstances it's what I would have liked.

That's the way it goes.

I like skiing.

Cross-country I mean.

Not downhill.

It's maybe something I've inherited from my mum.

Mum was really good at skiing.

Neither boys nor girls could keep up with her.

She raced against Toini Gustafsson once
and beat her.

She still has the cutting from the paper
about it.

The fellow who ran IK Likenäs, the ski club
wanted Mum to carry on
because she had talent.

But love intervened
and no more came of it.

Dad worked in Ruskåsen for many years
cutting timber for the parish.

The fornication forest.

The forest owned by the church.

We're coming to a sensitive chapter now
and I don't know if it's true
but it wouldn't surprise me.

If a farmer had a daughter
who became pregnant
and they didn't know who the father was
then the child was a bastard.

If they had any assets
the church would take them as a fine.

Because it was a sin
to have illegitimate children.

Fines for not following God's law.

That's what's written in my dad's birth certificate.

Illegitimate.

And Järnbergsås.

That's where I come from.

My mum was born there.

It's a long story.

They woke up one morning
and two of the boys had gone.

No one knew
but they showed up after the estate inventory.

They found their descendants
in Norway.

They just ran away.

They were starving.

Think about it . . . ten children
and there were no child benefits
or anything of that sort.

Same with Vålberg
over beyond Ruskåsen.

My granny and grandpa took in two boys
so they could attend school.

Hugo and Tore.

When it was the school summer holiday
they were supposed to go back.

But when the minister came
to fetch them
they ran off and hid.

Grandpa said
Let them stay then.

They stayed until they were called up for national service.

They never ever went back home.

They didn't want to go home.

Their home was
with me.

There were seven of us living
in two rooms and kitchen.

They didn't have any food.

Twelve brothers and sisters.

And Grandpa told me
they were barefoot when they came.

We did have food, though
even during the war years.

We had lots of food.

Others didn't have any.

They came on their bikes, they did
from small places like Hagfors . . .
there was nothing there then.

They came on bikes at night
and begged for food.

At our butchery.

There were coupons, of course.

Even the minister
tried to fiddle things
according to what my grandfather told me.

Tapped on the bedroom window.

In order to please Mum
I got a job at the post office in Karlstad.

I didn't find school difficult
and was expected to make something of myself
in the post office or a bank.

I knew it wasn't for me
but did it anyway
because it was what Mum wanted.

The post office was on Kungsgatan
and I lived on Drottninggatan.

I found my way to Kungsgatan
where the post office was by the church
but they showed me out on the other side.

I came out down by the canal in Haga
and I'll be buggered
if I could find my way home.

There weren't any trees
or hills and rocks
as I was used to.

No one had bothered to tell me
to look up at the corner of the streets.

Eventually a taxi came along
I stopped the taxi
and asked if she would take me
to 40 Drottninggatan.

Of course, she said
but why don't you just walk across the street?

Nitro Metal, that was in Likenäs.

They used explosive welding to produce metals
for space craft, ice-breakers, anything you care to name.

We'd lay one sheet of metal
on top of another
and spread explosive material
over the whole of the sheet
before detonating it.

Anything up to eight hundred kilos of explosive.

It bonds them together.

Forms a plasma jet between them.

We even detonated silver.

Titanium.

For spacecraft.

In order to pass through the atmosphere
the cladding
is bonded from sheets of that sort.

Nuclear reactors
in that case it's silver and steel.

Ice-breakers
in that case it's titanium and steel.

I don't know
whether to tell you about these things.

If you think
it's of no use to you
you can just cut it.

These are the kind of materials
they use now
the terrorists, I mean.

Fertiliser, salt and diesel.

To make explosives.

We live in the middle of the forest.

That's your raw material.

It's bloody ridiculous
that a sheet of chipboard
can't be produced at a profit.

That it's more profitable to fell the timber here
and transport it five hundred miles.

They're not exactly thinking about the environment.

We've got sawmills.

Capable of processing timber
making mouldings
doing everything.

But it isn't done.

Everything has to be transported somewhere else.

Think of Branäs.

Their headquarters is in Karlstad
and that's where they pay tax.

There's almost no one from here
working for Branäs.

Think of the chipboard . . .
taxed in Östersund.

Think of all the people who've inherited forest here
but live somewhere else.

They make a profit from the forests here
and then pay tax where they live.

In Gothenburg
or in Stockholm.

Think of the power stations.

They pay their taxes in Örebro and Stockholm.

Because that's where they have their headquarters.

When I was at Gammelbyn holiday village
I used to sell elk shit.

Twenty-five kronor a bag
small plastic bags
just one litre.

Elk shit.

And every single warning sign about elk just disappeared.

They had to shoot holes through the signs
to give them a chance of them being left in place.

They'd be left where they were then.

It stops the Germans turning them into tables.

I come from a family
that showed aggression
as well as love and tenderness.

If you're given love and tenderness
you can put up
with a clip round the ear.

As far as I'm concerned
a clip round the ear isn't assault
but a clenched fist
certainly is.

I've not been any the worse for it.

It was a marker
that enough is enough.

What do you do
when talking no longer helps?

I never thought Mum was being nasty.

The only thing she did wrong
was that she never explained
why she was angry.

Grandpa used to do it instead.

Take me by the hand
round behind the wall
and tell me why Mum was angry.

He's with me every day.

I once phoned from Karlstad
I lived in Karlstad for many years
and it was Grandpa who answered.

I'm coming home at the weekend.

That'll be good
we can cut the logs.

I was a bit wild then
and always looking for the heaviest work
which was rolling the logs up
on to the sawing table.

I came to a pretty hefty log
and fumbled it
so it crashed down.

Since the table was empty
I picked up a smaller log
to give the cutters something to do.

We'll give you a hand, Grandpa yelled.

No! No! Keep cutting!

In the end Grandpa switched off the saw
and took me by the shoulder.

Sit down here boy, he said.

I was really botching lifting that bloody log.

Sit down here boy, he said.

We sat down
and he looked me straight in the eye.

Now look, he said
You know, don't you, that we work to survive.

Yes, I said
We do.

So why go working yourself to death?
he said.

He thought I was behaving stupidly.

I started the folk-dance team in Ekshärad.

No matter what
when you are dealing with people
and want them to learn something
whether it's dancing or sports . . .

Point number one
is that it should be fun.

But some people
put the cultural side
at number one.

That ruins it for me.

The idea that you must have
the right clothes for folk dancing
for this century or that century . . .

The fun has gone out of it by that point.

I never drink spirits
when I need to act as leader for something
and I've always finished
anything I've agreed to take on.

But I was criticised for
drinking spirits
and whooping and stamping my feet
when dancing
because the books don't tell us that they used to do that.

So I asked them
What's a dance team for then?

Well, it's to preserve local culture.

In that case, I said,
I must be thinking along the right lines
because we've been boozing and stamping our feet in Ekshärad
ever since the beginning of time.

It was part of the Youth Association, you see.

I've got my own home-distilling set-up at home
I said
which probably makes me the most cultured of the lot of you.

Now if it's all right with you I've nothing to add.

That was the last thing I ever did
for the Youth Association.

I went to Africa
and Ronny Styffe came with us
he's a mate of ours
a mutual friend.

Everybody thought we were going there to hunt
but we weren't.

We wanted to see something different.

We're not interested in places like Kos or Mallorca
and all those beaches.

Drinking, swimming, sunbathing
we can do all that at home.

We've got the same sun here in Osebol
and the booze is the same
so why should we bother to go there.

We wanted to see something different
And we visited a town called Kitale.

Someone there had a couple of enormous speakers.

The treble crackled and hissed
but I picked up the beat
triple time.

Bugger this, I said
once I get out of this shop
I'm going to dance.

Go on said Ronny
Go ahead and let's see what happens.

No don't, Annika said
Don't
the police will come.

It was still the same noise when I went out
so I put down the bags
and started dancing.

Hallingdans steps.

Loads of people gathered round
it was a public square, after all.

And the police arrived.

With whips
to hold the people back.

And guess what?
I was a celebrity
from then on.

Do you know what I was thinking
while I did it?

I was thinking
What if I'd done the same thing
outside the Toria supermarket in Torsby?

If I was sober
they'd come and take me away every time.

If I was drunk
and behaved like that
no one would react.

Some people felt sorry for Annika
for getting together with a ruffian like me.

I don't know why.

Maybe it's because
I'm not like many other people
who just agree with the previous speaker.

If I think something is wrong
I speak out.

I'm stupid enough
to think it's great
that people are different.

Think
what it would be like if you and I were the same
what would we have to talk about?

The fact we are different
is the icing on the cake in my opinion.

I don't want to end up
spending my time acting a part
I want to be myself.

I was on the Gammelbyn reception desk one afternoon.

It was due to close at six o'clock
when along came a crowd of kids.

Tell us about the forest, will you?

Not now . . . I have customers
but come back at six o'clock.

And they came back.

I shut the reception
but left the door open
and sat down on the sofa by the wall
which was there for customers
along with a table and some armchairs.

So that's where I sat.

Right then, what do you want me to tell you?

Tell us about the wolf.

I sat there and told them the story.

They were all ears.

I had to tell a few lies of course
to make it really exciting.

Two little ones came up to me
and looked at me.

Do you want to sit on my knee? I said.

Yes.

I lifted them up on my knee
and carried on with the story.

Then up came two mothers
furious with the children and with me.

And told them
they mustn't go sitting on the knee
of men they didn't know
and gave me a bawling out as well.

I thought then
What kind of attitude towards older people
are these children being given?

I was at one of the most beautiful places in Värmland.

It's called Lake Mangen.

And I'm standing there looking
and then I think
My God, is everything ready?

I looked at the papers
and checked things off.

Restaurant, food,
horses, motor bikes,
the whole caboodle.

The cabins were ready
the canoes were ready.

I looked at the clock.

My God, is everything really ready?

And there's still forty-five minutes
before they're due to arrive.

I checked the book several times.

Yes, it's all ready.

In which case I'll go and have a bite . . .
I'll take my bag
and sit down by the lake.

And while I was sitting there
I broke down
and went home.

I cried so much
I barely managed to get home.

I've never been back there since.

That's what happened.

I think some good comes of it
when you hit rock bottom
and are lucky enough to work your way back up.

It changes you.

It makes you more humble
and happier
just to wake up in the morning
when you're nearly seventy
able to get yourself up
and feed yourself
and wipe your own backside.

Because there's no bloody guarantee
you'll be able to do it.

But then she fell ill.

I can tell you
ten years of our life
was quite simply hell.

When my wife said
I've got cancer
I must go home and pack . . .

That's when I saw the abyss
and I
came crashing down.

This is it.

But it was good, too
in that it reminded me
I still loved her.

I'd forgotten that.

That's how things are.

If everything
is just good, good, good
in the end you stop remembering
how good your life is.

It does you good sometimes
to get a slap in the face
so you wake up and realise
just how bloody good your life is.

I had Ida with me
and just before we reached Bränna
a wolf came running down
the hillside out onto the road.

At first Ida thought it was a reindeer.

I said
No, my God it's a wolf.

She was afraid and wanted to turn back
and go straight home.

I said
I'm just going to go and have a look
at the size of its pawprints.

They were really big.

They were the size of your hand
and it was muddy so they showed up.

It was probably
just as frightened as we were.

The dog didn't make a sound.

There aren't any elk.

Not in huntable numbers.

It's a result of hunting and wolves.

I've given up hunting
because of the wolves.

We have to go and buy old food now
wrapped in plastic in the shop.

I hate it.

I want to know what I'm eating.

I have nine roe deer that I'm feeding here.

Here comes the little goat.

They're mean to it.

See the one up there, at the edge of the trees
do you see how small she is?

She's not allowed to come down.

It's because of their pecking order.

She's only allowed to come down once the others have eaten.

Are they still there?

                              Yes, they're driving the little goat away.

                              She had to run up there and stop.

They've grown more now, the antlers.

                              Yes, that's the old buck.

                              And there's one more buck up there.

One year we had a buck
with such a fine crown on him.

We watched the whole time
right from when it began growing.

I said, Imagine if we found those antlers . . .
because they do drop them, of course.

                              One, two, three, four, five, six, seven
                              and there are two over there.

                              There are two standing under the spruce tree.

Annika Axelsson b. 1959
316 | *Åke Axelsson b. 1947*

I told my workmates
I'd bought a holiday home.

I said it's in Osebol.

No one in Stockholm had heard of the place.

Near Stöllet, I told them.

No one has heard of that either.

They think it sounds funny.

Are you crazy, like?

I tell them it's in the Torsby district.

They don't know where that is either.

I say Branäs.

At last they begin to get some vague idea.

Most of my friends and colleagues
do a lot of travelling.

They go abroad a lot.

Buying a holiday home
in northern Värmland
makes you a strange bird.

Most of them travel
to the Alps for the skiing
or to holiday resorts
in the USA, Mexico, Thailand
and god knows where else.

And I come here.

The scenery here is dramatic.

There's the low land
and then the river
and steep mountain sides.
and the houses . . .

It's very special.

Maybe
a little bit of me
bought the house here
as a kind of protest.

I know that buying a holiday home
is not right.

I ought to move here.

If you use it as a holiday home
you're actually encouraging the depopulation.

Some days I find it a real struggle
to manage in Stockholm.

Getting to and from work
takes an enormous amount of time.

I don't have a car
and I use public transport.

It takes the best part of an hour
door to door.

The undergound is crowded
and there are delays
the moment we have some snow . . .
it gets on your nerves.

I grew up in Kristinehamn.

I never thought
I'd end up in Stockholm.

And I didn't think
I'd stay.

I've lived there
almost nine years now.

The fact is it's much easier
to get a job there.

I'm an IT consultant.

It's important for me
to have good connectivity.

In my old job
I had the possibility
of working from home.

You connect to servers
and the customers' data systems.

That opens up possibilities to live here
in a very different way.

I'm about to start
a new job now.

If the customer wants you
to be present the whole time
there's not much to be done about it.

But sometimes the customer
is short of office space
and doesn't want you sitting there.

It's hard to say
but obviously
it's more difficult
if you can't get fibre broadband.

As you approach from the south
you see the bridge
with the church tower in the middle.

I said to Petra
We must take a photo of that
and put it on the internet.

It turned out that
exactly the same photo already exists.

                    The Norra Ny area development association
                               has a Facebook group.

                    They already have that picture
                         of the arches of the bridge
                                 and the church.

Jörgen Lange b. 1942
326 | Petra Lange b. 1978

Nystugan
do you know anything about its history?

It was a fellow called Jon Halvardsson
who had the big house built
but he ran into financial difficulties
and had to give up everything.

There was a good deal of booze
involved.

He bought it by the crate.

In addition to bad business deals.

He may have stood surety
for someone who couldn't pay up.

The place was auctioned off
and then they bought a house
north of here.

He lived there as long as he could
then did up the stable
and ended up living in that.

The stable is still there.

Straight across from István's stable.

That's where he lived
and he could look across to what used to be his
on the other side of the road.

Daniel at Sandvik
had a kiosk and filling station
on the main square in Osebol.

The kiosk was yellow outlined with red.

It stood on the corner
and had a metal cupboard for cans of oil and the like
as well as the actual petrol pump.

Before we got TV
that's where all the local men used to get together
almost every evening
to chat about anything and everything.

It must have still been there
into the sixties.

It was still there
when I had a moped.

There was business activity
at Ekberg's as well.

He was a timber buyer
for the Wargön company . . .
Folke, I mean.

He employed loggers and
was in charge of getting the timber out.

Olle Ekberg ran the Gästis Hotel in Stöllet
and later the Väbergsstugan restaurant.

My father was a forestry worker.

When he started he felled trees by hand
and later worked with a chainsaw.

Worked mainly for Folke Ekberg.

They had to be debarked as well.

That was OK when the temperature was above zero
but when it went below freezing in winter
things got really hard . . .
well, you can imagine . . .
the barking iron bounced off the bark.

When the weather was at its coldest
you couldn't do more than a centimetre or so at a time.

My mother was a housewife.

She never worked outside the home.

We had two or three cows
as well as pigs and sheep.

That was more than enough to deal with.

And seeing about the hay.

She was out in the fields with us whenever she could.

Now and again someone might come
and buy a litre of milk
otherwise it was mostly for our household needs.

We took the grain
to the Värå mill
and got it ground to flour.

Things got smaller and smaller.

For a while towards the end
we had one cow.

That was most likely sometime in the seventies.

Then we had to get by without the cow.

It was a change, of course
though I think they were quite happy with it.

We did have a cow here
when the new people came to Nystugan.

They were quite curious
about the fact there was a cow.

There was a commune there at that point.

It was quite unusual
for there to be so many people living there.

And the appearance of some of them!

I've carried on
with my electrical bits and pieces here.

I taught myself.

It all started
with me taking all kinds of things to bits
when I was small.

There weren't many things
I could leave alone . . .
I always had to be tinkering with something.

And then there'd be something wrong with a radio
and I'd try to mend it
and I got better and better at it.

I read all the books I could get hold of
about that kind of thing.

And then there was the whole business
of electrical faults in cars.

Someone came to me
with a generator that wouldn't charge.

I started by repairing that
and things mushroomed from there.

Rewinding coils for electric motors and the like.

They're made up of a mass of copper wire
wound in a tight coil
and lacquered for insulation.

If something causes it to run hot
the lacquer burns off.

That means the coil wires
are no longer insulated against each other.

Which means they have to be ripped out
and replaced with new wire.

When I started I didn't have premises
but then I bought this shed
and turned it into my workshop.

When the chipboard factory was set up
I got plenty of work
rewinding the motors.

One or more burned out almost daily.

The ones that powered the machines in the factory
saws and polishing machines
anything and everything.

My business was called Radio & Elmechanical.

I still have it
though it doesn't do much these days.

I've been a pensioner for ten years.

No, there was the move to Malung, of course.

It was at Solvik
at an ordinary dance.

The long holiday weekend
autumn eighty-nine.

She was out celebrating
becoming a grandmother.

In the beginning
I went over at weekends
and then midweek as well
and later more or less the whole time.

For quite some time I used to drive back here
to work during the day . . .
drive back and forth.

But then, of course, Inger became ill.

That calendar up there
the one still up on the wall
is for December two thousand and eight.

That must be the last year she came here with me.

Otherwise
a new calendar
would probably have been put up.

If you need anything
there's a lot more to be had in Malung.

Shops where you can get hold of
anything you want
without any bother.

But at the same time . . .
this is where home is, isn't it.

I'll probably stay there over the winter.

She has two boys, Inger does,
and they've said I can stay on.

It's nice
that they think like that.

But I do want to get this house
in order, too.

Sometimes when I'm here
I think I should be in Malung
and vice versa.

We'll have to see.

This is Birgit's electoral register from sixty-one.

Her father was on the polling station staff.

So he had it.

Andersson, Bror Vilhelm, forestry worker . . .
that was my dad, that was.

And Andersson, Elin Kristina, née Nilsson . . .
that was my mum.

He was born in Röjden, in Södra Finnskoga parish.

It was because of the UAB
they had in the 1930s.

Unemployment Assistance Boards.

They were building roads here
and he stayed on.

This is her parental home
in a manner of speaking.

She was actually Björ's daughter
you know
then her mum died.

Elin was two or three years old
when they took her in here
because the man of the house, Per Grund
was her mother's brother
and they had no children.

So she always referred to
Per Grund as Dad
though he was actually her uncle.

Her father's name was Nils Persson Björ.

He was the allotted soldier for Björby
which is why his name was Björ.

They had to take the name
of the village they represented.

The one in Osebol
didn't want to be called Os
so he called himself Ås
and Asp.

There are two different theories
about the name Osebol.

The accepted one
is that someone called Åsa
lived here
and that's what the name derives from.

But 'os'
can mean the mouth of a river, can't it
and some people claim
that the Stöa burn which now runs
straight into the river at Stödalen
used to flow south
through this village.

I don't know which is right.

There were fifteen shops in the parish of Norra Ny
when I was small.

And people didn't buy so much in those days
since they kept animals
and were self-sufficient.

The spirit of the times was different.

Things didn't have to produce a big profit.

People were easier to please
and things were calmer.

Not so much of a hurry.

Not everyone wanted to have it all
and not everyone was willing to spend their time
chasing enough money to get it.

Many people had some kind of smallholding
and they could get work in the forest in winter.

They stayed home during the summer
and that worked too, somehow.

They didn't fell trees in the summer.

The trees could be affected
by insects and mould
and turn blue.

It goes on all year round now.

No timber's left lying any more.

Chainsaws were introduced
and other forest machinery
and everything had to be done faster and faster
even though not much needed
to be done by hand.

People started buying cars
and driving around.

And then there were holiday trips.

There wasn't much travelling
anywhere at all
on our part.

There wasn't.

I suppose we went to a few events
in the immediate vicinity.

I'm not a member of the fibre association.

In Malung we got an old computer
from Hans, Inger's boy,
but I've never learnt to use it.

If I were to use a computer
it would be for making payments
and looking up technical things . . .
finding wiring diagrams
for whatever I happened to be working on.

For things like that
you can get by with wireless broadband.

And who knows what the future will bring.

In five, ten years
maybe fibre will be old hat.

I still use old-fashioned giro for my payments.

That means driving over to the Nordea Bank in Torsby
now and again.

They used to have a branch in Malung
but they've moved it to Mora
so the notice said.

As if they hadn't had
a branch in Mora before.

There was a note pinned on the door.

We have moved our branch to Mora.

Not we've closed down the Malung branch.

That would have looked worse.

Not many people
use cash.

They've taken away
the cash dispenser
which used to be at Hotel Värmlandsporten.

I'm in Malung often enough
and can withdraw money there
but it's not ideal.

Charities
selling prize draw tickets . . .
how are they supposed to deal with it?

What would happen
if we had
a long electricity cut?

If that happens you won't be able to use
anything apart from cash . . .
if that.

We looked at a place
down near Skymnäs
and at the same time drove up
and had a look at Bränna.

Per and Marie
friends down at Eftnäs
tipped us off that it was going.

Edla died first
and then Ville
and it still wasn't . . .

It's pretty overgrown now
because I haven't been able to keep it clear.

We lived near Per and Marie.

There used to be a way down
that was OK as a path.

It got washed away in eighty-seven.

I've never seen
so much rain
apart from in the tropics.

The road disappeared in the autumn.

Four-metre potholes opened up
since it was built on sand.

Partly our fault, no doubt . . .
we should have paid some attention to it
and the drainage
and keeping it open.

That's what Ville would have done.

We blew it.

Or I did.

When we moved up here
we started growing things
potatoes, carrots and onions
jointly with other people.

We made use of each other's ground.

Got together
did the weeding
and earthed up the potatoes.

We kept pigs too.

Everyone was complaining about pork
and how bad it tasted
how bad it was.

The pigs we kept
were free-range.

We did our own slaughtering here on the farm
with a slaughterman.

My brother took some of it
as did other people down in town.

Some people bought it
they had to bloody pay though.

They used to say
this tastes like real pork
just like when we were small.

I grew up
at the end of the forties
beginning of the fifties
before artificial fertilisers
and sprays came in.

When I was a small child . . .
we bought our potatoes from a farm
up in the hills.

The almond potatoes grown
down on the coast around Umeå
weren't good enough for Dad.

There was a hill farmer
he bought from
and drove out there to collect them.

I'm one of the last generations
to be spared that sort of thing.

Allergies and the like.

I doubt I knew a single sufferer.

It was extremely unusual.

When I started at Sysslebäck
there were almost two hundred pupils
without a nursery level
or a primary level.

When I finished there ten years later
there were a hundred and twenty, hundred and forty
and that included all ten levels.

About seven years into that period
Björklund stabbed schools in the back
by saying
we had the worst schools in the world.

That turned the whole community of parents
against the schools
particularly parents whose children had difficulties.

Aha, so it wasn't my fault then!

It was the school that got it wrong.

We had some pupils
we went and fetched in the morning.

Their parents couldn't get them to go to school.

It wasn't our job
but people took it on.

We took the view
or tried to take it
that all children are everyone's children.

Even if they have parents of their own
they are still the children of society as a whole.

I think
that's a good basic outlook.

Counselling and administrative staff
were cut back.

When I finished
there weren't any staff
of any kind
who were at the school
every day of the week.

Not even the dinner ladies
were there every day . . .
they had two schools
and alternated between them.

The headteacher was only there
maybe two days a week
just a half day each time.

He had two or three other schools
to go to as well.

The cleaning staff
are really important to a school.

We had a fantastic team of cleaners.

Children come in and
chuck everything around
just as they do at home . . .
down on the floor
in the corridors in winter.

So they really are important
plus there's the fact that they patrol the corridors
and see everything.

It's all about continuity.

When I started
there were posts in both careers advice
and counselling.

When I finished
there was just one person
looking after both counselling and careers.

She covered four schools.

Distances being long, she and the headteachers
spent thirty, forty percent of the working week
driving their cars.

It's thirty miles
between the schools in Klarälvdale
and then over to Fryksdale
or Ljusnandale
that's where Vitsand is.

It takes a great deal of time.

And sitting in your car without any relaxation
is really wearing.

I don't think I'm cut out
to be a politician.

It just makes me furious
that they can be so stupid
and incapable of seeing what's best.

And I have difficulty
signing up to any ideology.

All ideologies and religions
look wonderful
on paper.

When they are describing
how you should be and what you should do.

But the simple fact is no one sticks to the rules.

And those who break the rules
are rewarded.

Then divorces increased.

Divorce is very common here
just like everywhere else.

Single mothers
for the most part.

There are some
single fathers too
but not many.

But there are fathers
who do their bit
there really are.

But by and large . . .

I think
sex roles are more rigid here.

Maybe that's what happens
when circumstances are tougher.

We thought we were going to meet
rosy-cheeked children
who got up in the morning
drove the cows out to pasture
went back for a wholesome plate of porridge
and came to school full of . . .

But they were pale, apathetic.

I haven't slept.

So what do you do in the evening?

I sit up snacking and chatting
to Mum and Dad.

Well, I mean . . .
if they're filling themselves with coffee
and cream and sugar and buns
at ten or eleven at night . . .

Far too many of them arrived at school
exhausted wrecks.

That was a disappointment.

I thought it was going to be healthier
than it was.

What's more I discovered
that drinking, just drinking
was an activity in its own right.

I realised that after a while.

People at work would say
Come the weekend we'll do some drinking.

People might turn up in the evening
bottle in hand.

Walk in
sit down at the kitchen table
and pour drinks.

The first five, ten years anyway.

As long as I was working
and wasn't
so to speak, in quote marks
one of the intellectuals.

They would talk
and I'd try to stay with it
and understand what they were saying . . .
dialect and the like.

Then I'd look . . .
But who's that sitting out in the car?

That's the wife
the old lady
was what they usually said.

Doesn't she want to come in for coffee?

She was acting as chauffeur of course.

No, she'd rather stay there.

And then I began to understand
why the children had
such unbelievably rigid ideas
about the roles of the sexes.

Segregation is extremely marked.

Those who own the forests
and have money
usually grandparents on the mother's or father's side
obviously their kid
needs a scooter.

So they go and buy one, cash down
pull out their fat wallet
and count out twenty-five, thirty . . .
It costs forty-five
Right, OK . . .
thousand.

And off they go home
with a scooter or a quadbike
while the rest just stand and watch.

The class divisions I encountered
when I came here were enormous.

Those who have
and those who don't.

Those who rent
and those who own
you might say.

And then there's the business of them and us.

I think I was
accepted quite well
and Tina was too in the end
though it was more difficult for her.

This whole business of sex roles
is very strong.

Men and women simply
don't socialise together.

Luckily for us
there were back-to-the-land types
or groups of hippies
living in the area.

Most of our socialising was with them.

Almost all of them had children
and two or three families
would drop in on a fourth family.

Children's activities were the thing
there was no drinking
no boozing
no alcohol.

We would play football until it was time
for the kids to get their heads down
and there'd be a room
with ten children sleeping in it
and somebody reading.

That was our salvation.

That was our safety-valve
somewhere the children could play
with others of their own kind.

The first time
I came here
I sat and looked to the east.

It was summer
late summer.

Not a sound.

The wind was blowing
so you couldn't hear the traffic on the 62
on the other side of the river.

I felt peace.

Oh . . .
it opens out around you.

I still feel it
when I come home
after being in town.

Even so
I can easily picture myself
living in a little one-room flat
in the park by Teo's flat.

It would be close
to transport links
and above all
children and grandchildren.

But then . . .
I'm settled here.

Anyway I doubt
whether I'd recoup
the money I borrowed.

So . . . for the sake of the children
it's better if I die here.

If I understand it right
you can't inherit debts.

I don't know how many picture postcards
there are of Osebol bridge.

If you go round markets
they usually turn up.

At one place there was one
I'd never seen before.

It was priced at over two hundred kronor
so I handed it back.

Normally I'd pay
a tenner, maybe fifteen.

It's earmarked for demolition
but funds aren't currently available.

That's why they put up fences
which people then cut down.

It's to make you aware that you're crossing
at your own risk.

But walking across isn't dangerous.

I do it.

The circuit of the bridges
is a popular walk.

A lot of people go across and run it.

It's a sort of trademark for the whole district.

It'd be a pity if they were to demolish it.

A great pity.

There are fewer children
so our survival now
is dependent on refugees
the refugee accommodation at Värmlandsporten.

I've got thirteen children
six of them asylum seekers.

Obviously I was a bit anxious
when they first came.

We'd prepared our own children
in advance . . .
they're likely to be very frightened and shy
maybe won't say much
just stay close to the walls
and perhaps cry a lot.

And in came seven whirlwinds.

They found their feet from day one.

The downside
the only thing
that makes things a bit difficult
is that they . . .

They aren't here for long.

Three, maybe four months
and then there's a change.

That's hard.

You get attached to them, of course you do.

You read in the papers
about the boats crossing the Mediterranean
and the things that happen
but you can't take it in
still can't understand it.

And then suddenly you find yourself
sitting opposite a mother who
was actually there holding on
to her two-year old boy
so he wouldn't fall in.

That's when it becomes real.

In the beginning . . . when it first opened
a great many people got involved.

People would get together at the community centre
bake bread and cook meals.

But interest just faded away
when it became an everyday routine.

The old forestry school buildings
are used for unaccompanied refugee children.

There are a dozen or so boys from Afghanistan living there.

They feel they're stuck in the middle of the forest
and they're not too happy.

I'm the legal guardian of one of the boys.

He says
You have to help me
I have to get away from here.

I tell him I can't
that I'm not the one who decides.

I'll run away then he says.

I tell him it will just make things worse
because you'll be back to square one.

You sit there and . . .
it's a pity about this, a pity about that
and you do nothing about it.

What the hell I thought.

They were advertising for guardians and I thought
I can't say
I'm not up to it
if I haven't even tried.

When I took it on
there were three jobs to be done.

Applying for money and distributing it
being present at the first interview with the Immigration Office
being present at the first medical.

That was a whitewash if ever there was one . . .
there's a lot more to it than that.

You actually become a surrogate parent.

We have to learn from each other.

The young people
are the ones who suffer.

I have to go online and search the net
What do I do now?
What shall I do in this case?

Then staff at the residential centre ring up
Have you done it yet?

Shit
Was I supposed to do that too?

But you certainly learn.

In the beginning he was a calm and kind boy
who didn't say a lot
but he's been in Sweden nearly two years now
and nothing is happening.

He still hasn't been informed
whether he can stay.

You only have to look at them.

To see they're weary.

They want to know
what's going to happen.

Will I be allowed to stay?

It's also dawned on them
that Stöllet is very small.

It's a long way to school
a long way to any activities.

It gets to them
and I understand that.

But the question perhaps . . .

I think it's mainly emotional wear and tear
and that means that concrete issues . . .
things that are easy to put your finger on . . .

Whereas in reality it may well be
something else entirely.

He is clever.

He doesn't think he's clever
but he is clever.

If something doesn't suit him
his way of dealing with it
is not to know any Swedish.

He won't understand what I'm saying.

That's the situation.

They're no different from most youngsters.

He likes talking
about the town he comes from
and now he's confident enough to trust me
more and more emerges
about what he experienced
and that's what is so . . .

You read about child soldiers in the papers
and all of a sudden you understand
Yes, that's what it's really like.

I didn't use to have any idea about
things like asylum applications
and what a hard process it turns out to be.

Presumably that's because so many
arrived at the same time.

Sweden as a whole was
taken by surprise and shocked.

And then . . .
I don't really know
but I suspect that
the knowledge of the higher-ups
maybe wasn't . . .

They didn't know
because they'd never had
this experience before.

There won't be any more asylum seekers
staying at Värmlandsporten
after the beginning of September.

It'll feel strange.

It's been in use for four years.

All of us . . . the school,
the shop, the filling station
will see a difference.

It's become a feature of the district.

Part of the local picture.

They always look happy walking down the road
waving hello.

We'd hoped
more of them would stay
but many of them say
they'd have considered staying
if it wasn't for the issue of job opportunities.

They don't grow on trees.

If I've got my arithmetic right . . .
in south Stöllet
there are now fifteen children
as well as a number of adults
and otherwise it's all old people's flats.

Many of the older generation
say that Stöllet has come alive again.

It certainly wasn't before.

You don't see youngsters out on their bikes
these days.

They've started going out a bit more
thanks to Pokémon Go.

But these young people are out cycling . . .
out walking.

So it's a real pity.

I understand that fewer
will be getting into Sweden.

But I do think
some thought could be given to rural areas.

Anna-Karin Larsson b. 1972 | *397*

The house was built in nineteen thirty-six
by Johannes, my father's father.

His brother Axel
was still living in the old Törnsgårn
and grandfather built this house next to it.

After Dad passed away
in nineteen ninety-two
we divided things up
so this was one property
and the other a separate one.

The name of this house is Broby
but no one ever uses it
they still say Törnsgårn
for both of them.

It had never really entered my head
to move here.

The idea of moving
back to this house.

But when my brother Staffan passed away
I thought that maybe it shouldn't be left empty.

I'm not the domestic sort.

I'm completely unpractical
can't do anything
hate shovelling snow
and hate cutting grass.

I really ought to be living in a flat
but I'm living here now
and there's no point thinking about it
you can only take things as they are.

Late one evening last autumn
I was about to turn off the light in the TV room.

But then I thought
Goodness me, have I watered the flowers?

The window ledge was soaking wet.

It was raining cats and dogs outside
and the rain was coming in
and I wondered
What am I going to do now?

I phoned my cousin
Sven-Åke.

There's water coming in at the window.

Is it coming from above?
he said.

Obviously it's coming from above!

Bugger
he shouted.

Put down the phone
I'll come over straightaway.

His first thought was
there was a fault with a radiator
upstairs.

Once I took over the house
everything really became settled.

Now this is where you live.

I found it hard work at first
but the more time passes
the more I can sit back.

What the hell
it's just a house.

I grew up here
and I've lived here
but it's still just a house.

We'll have to see what happens.

When I was young
and there were plenty of people around to ask
I wasn't interested.

But now that I've begun to think
a bit about family and kin . . .
there's no one left to ask.

I've changed round the kitchen and bathroom now . . .
it occurs to me
that it was probably Dad who decided
the way it was.

But I don't give it a lot of thought.

Most of the time I wonder
how they could have been so stupid
as to build the house this way?

Doors everywhere.

But then . . .

I'm sometimes grateful
they built it
exactly where they did.

When you look
over to the west of me
there's no sun
it's all in shade.

I have sun the whole day
morning to evening.

I often talk to Monica about it
each of us in our own place on a Saturday evening
with a glass of wine perhaps
and sending texts
and commenting
on something we've seen on TV.

Did you watch that?

That's what people do.

It's a bit like that now.

Everyone taken up with their own stuff.

It's dreadful really.

I don't think it used to be like that.

Or maybe it was
because people used to have less to do
I don't know.

It's different in summer.

It's as if you can do more.

You can get out your bike.

Be more sociable.

Visit people's houses.

Everything is much easier in the summer.

I went to Malmö for the first time
last year . . . in the summer.

It was great
just to get on the train
and in no time at all
we were in Copenhagen

We went to Christiania.

I was really astonished.

They were standing there in balaclavas and gloves
selling.

I've kept one of those bucket lists.

Places I want to go to.

Christiania was one of them.

The Hornborga Lake was on it too.

I went there last year.

Nineteen thousand one hundred cranes.

Easter Island's also on the list.

The question is
whether I'm still interested in going there.

I was quite young when I wrote the list.

The last time we talked
it was winter and miserable.

At the time my feeling was
No, I shan't be staying here.

But when all's said and done
I feel that living here is rather nice
now summer is coming.

And you can sort of feel . . .
I'm thinking of Stockholm last Friday . . .
living here in the country
is nice and peaceful after all.

There's a feeling of security here too.

And you have a social network.

I find it hard to imagine
anyone else living here.

After all, it's my house.

I'm in two minds.

I wish there were a reasonable compromise.

There's also the fact
maybe more than you care to admit
that here you are somebody.

If you move somewhere else
you'll become totally anonymous.

I was visiting
a work colleague
and his wife
and we talked about Sweden.

I said
We really should go there.

We'd never been here before.

We said
Oh, we love the silence
we love the nature.

I've always loved Emil.

I saw him on T V
and felt really close
to that little boy.

I was a bit like him.

I was always outdoors
and I played with a knife.

I think it was my childhood . . .
with Emil and Sweden.

I was six, seven, eight.

I'm forty-five now.

At the end of the trip
we just had to buy the house.

It had to be.

Back in Holland we live in a place
a bit like this.

Out in the country too.

There's no need to travel anywhere
in the summer.

It's nice at home then.

But we love winter sports
and they're expensive.

Prices are low here
compared with Holland.

We decided
not to go to Austria again.

We're spending our money on this place now
rather than on hotels.

It'll pay for itself in ten years.

Friends and family can visit us
and we can go skiing in Branäs.

We're missing one cat.

Two months ago in June.

I think something must have taken him
somewhere out there.

He was always allowed to roam free
which is good.

They like coming with us
want to be up in our laps
every evening.

They are with us here.

We're going to try to see
whether he can retire early
and get an early pension.

We'd be able to live on that here
once the house is paid off.

The two of us and a couple of animals.

We don't need much.

You can pick berries in the forest
and catch fish.

We have a barn.

We could maybe keep a cow
or a pig.

The old-fashioned way.

You feed them
until they're a year or two old.

Then we'd get some quality meat.

And know the animal has been well-treated.

I'll try to find a job.

They asked me about the fire and rescue service
but I'd need good Swedish for that.

I know that
because when I was in the police
and people got panicky
you really needed to know the language.

Doing it in English is not enough.

It'll take me two maybe three years
to learn Swedish that well.

Or perhaps I could help people
twenty-four hours a day
as I did in my last years in Holland.

I like that too.

And I can work in Branäs.

It doesn't really matter
as long as it's a job of some sort.

We tried to start a business.

We were going to have canoes
fishing and walking tours.

We'd lay on trips
for companies in Holland.

We called it Basic Sweden.

Our slogan was
Men Stay Boys.

We got hold of stickers
and had a number of bicycles.

But then he had a meeting with the colleague
he runs a furniture business with
and we had to choose.

And the furniture business it was!

We tried running a shop in the barn.

Furniture, antiques
axes, knives.

It didn't go too well
since around here
anyone who owns a table
inherited it from their parents
and will keep it sixty years.

People don't buy new furniture.

We've heard
it's possible to make a lot of money
doing this sort of thing
in Stockholm.

But we don't want to move to Stockholm.

We left Holland
because we liked it here.

Annemarie den Heijer b. 1971
Rick Keulen b. 1957 | 423

Doing business here
is difficult for people
from abroad
since we don't know the language that well.

Swedes are suspicious
and prefer buying things
from other Swedes.

It's easier in Holland.

When I advertise on the net there
I get responses.

People ask the size of the item
how much it costs
what colour it is.

I don't get any responses here.

Since we aren't very far
from Oslo and Karlstad
we thought
people might travel the hundred and twenty miles
to look at a table.

We've discovered they think it's too far.

And if they think it's too far they don't get in contact.

Rick Keulen b. 1957
424 | *Annemarie den Heijer b. 1971*

During that time
I painted the house.

I had no choice
but to stay here.

In case someone wanted to come
and look round.

So I painted the whole house.

We really did try.

There were problems with the car
on my way to the petrol station.

When I was driving back
it just stopped
right outside their house.

Åke came out
and tried to help me.

He's a mechanic.

But the engine was completely kaput.

That's how we met Åke.

> When we come up here in the winter . . .
> we have a long path down to the road
> and we can't plough it
> when we're not here.

He clears the snow
so we can get up here.

Rick Keulen b. 1957
426 | *Annemarie den Heijer b. 1971*

I stayed here for two stretches
during twenty eleven.

I had a sabbatical year.

I was here for five months
thinking about
what I wanted to do with my life.

What kind of work I wanted to do.

I was here a long time and then . . .

Annika and Åke
sort of became
my Swedish parents.

When I'm here
they're my parents.

Driving up from Holland
is eight hundred and seventy miles
one way.

He works with the furniture business down there . . .
they're very keen on kitchen settles in Holland.

This one is great.

I bought it online through Blocket, the online market.

People don't want this sort of thing anymore.

We'll take it to pieces
put it in the car
and we'll sell it
in our friend's shop.

It'll be the third time we've done that
this year.

It'll pay for the journey.

I think I'll paint this one white.

White with roses.

I think that will sell better
than brown.

Last time we found a really good settle
in Karlstad.

We picked it up
on our way home.

We didn't do anything
just put it in the car
and unloaded it from the car
and a woman from The Hague thought
Wow!

Geco and Ingrid
have an old settle.

I took a photo
and sent it to a factory in Romania.

They made the settle
and we sell it in Holland.

We call it the Klepbank Osebol.

The Osebol settle.

You can find it on the internet.

There's an interesting thing
about Osebol
that hadn't occurred to me
until now.

If this had been on
just about any river in Europe
the settlements would have
faced towards the river.

Had a little harbour.

It's the opposite here.

People here have always
been afraid of the river . . .
flooding and that sort of thing.

In all the settlements here
the houses face towards the road
then come fields and meadows
and then scrub
and then in the distance
there's the river.

The fact of it being a valley . . .
I think it's beautiful
especially the view down the valley.

But many people feel . . .
even in the commune they did . . .
lots of people weren't happy
because it felt confined.

Couldn't be doing with it.

Whereas others thought of it
as warm and protective.

What I remember from that time
is the way people lived.

We grew a lot of things.

The cottages around were occupied
by an older generation.

They were living a different life
a different way of life.

Out in the fields here
when it was time to bring in the hay
when it was dry
when it was time to build stooks . . .
these people
they had it in their blood.

They'd be waiting out on the veranda
in the morning
with rakes and what not
because it was time for the hay . . .

It was a different life.

We took in ours
and we took in theirs.

It goes without saying.

Same with the potato crop.

The fact of the matter was
that properly speaking
every patch of land
was owned by one or other of the oldies.

But when potatoes were grown
who actually owned them
became irrelevant
and people took what they needed.

In common.

People always pulled together.

We had horses
and we baked fantastic loaves at Christmas
with angels and things
we'd cut out and shaped.

I had plenty of rye flour
and raisins and cumin.

We made a great load
and harnessed up the horse and sledge
flaming torches
fiddles and accordions.

We went round farm to farm
handing out these Christmas loaves.

I was talking to my son
he lives in Stockholm now
in Västerhaninge
and I asked whether he could remember any of this.

They are really strong memories
from his childhood.

How could I not remember?
he says.

We arrived in Sweden
on the sixth of December nineteen fifty-six.

There were three buses from Austria
with refugees.

We crossed from Helsingör
to Helsingborg.

I stood at the front
as they lowered the ramp
to let us ashore.

I was taken by surprise
to see cars driving on the wrong side of the road.

They were still driving on the left.

All the cars moved over from the right
to the left
before driving on.

A handsome policeman in a dark blue uniform
with gold bits and a sabre
was standing on the quay.

We were impressed.

We saw something else
we'd never seen before
television aerials.

I'd never seen a television at all.

This was around the time
they were being introduced to Sweden.

The Hungarian Uprising . . .
why it made such an impression on people
why it was perceived in a different way
had a lot to do with TV, I think.

It was the first time you could see things live
things going on out in the world.

Before that there was only the radio.

We arrived in Helsingborg
and were driven to a place
that was presumably some sort
of hygiene establishment.

A kind of bathhouse
all small rooms and bathtubs.

If there was one thing they had plenty of
it was scrubbing brushes.

You'd never believe
how scrubbed and disinfected we were.

Then they threw away all the clothes
we were wearing.

These days it would be called
an invasion of privacy
but I suppose it was their way
of protecting themselves
and preventing filth coming in.

From there we were moved on to Falsterbo House.

Have you ever been down to Falsterbo?

There are these white beaches
and then this stunningly beautiful place
with stepped gables that looks like a Hanseatic house.

It's been converted
into a complex of luxury flats now
but it was a summer hotel in those days.

Since it was closed for the winter
we got to live in the hotel.

They employed cooks
and organised events
and I'm pretty sure
the king himself came and visited.

There was a positive sort of attitude
to the refugee issue at that time.

There was a labour shortage in Sweden in fifty-six.

I don't think we'd been there
more than a couple of days
before people started coming
from all sorts of industries.

That's how we met the family
to which I'm eternally grateful.

The Agrell family.

They owned the Addo calculating machine factory.

Things had gone amazingly well for them
and they needed more people for their factory.

They handpicked my mum and my sister
the whole family.

A close friendship developed out of it.

My God, they really helped us.

My father had been in Sweden
since nineteen forty-six.

During the war he'd walked on foot
all the way up to Sweden
because he had a brother there.

The intention was that
we would follow him
but then the Hungarian border was closed
and we couldn't go anywhere.

He was here for ten years without his family
and over the course of ten years
people tend to form other relationships.

And then we arrived.

The other individual
stepped aside
to allow the family to be reunited.

So we tried.

442 | *István Fóth b. 1943*

It worked for a few weeks
then things got harder.

After a month he wasn't coming for his meals . . .
my father.

My big sister was doing the cooking
when he hadn't come for supper
for a whole week.

She said
There's no point laying a place for dad
because he won't come anyway.

We didn't lay a place for him
that evening either
but then of course he turned up.

He saw a place hadn't been set for him
grabbed the saucepan of food
picked it up
and threw it
so that everything ended up on the ceiling.

Then he lined us up
Mum
big sister
little sister
me
and from left to right
each of us got a thick ear
and then he said
Out!

With just a Co-op bag in the middle of the night.

We spent the night with another refugee
and in the morning at the factory
Uncle Tryggve the director
sent for Mum.

Mum spoke pretty good German
and he spoke German quite well
he asked what the situation was
and what had happened.

Mum told him . . .
said that things were not great.

Then he said
Don't worry Mrs Fóth
I'll see what we can do.

He came back
and said that if Mrs Fóth would like
to go home and collect her children
and the Co-op bag
I'll come and pick you all up
at five o'clock.

So a really fancy BMW rolled up.

He didn't say much.

We arrived at a very grand block
right opposite the public park
on Amiralsgatan in Malmö
and he said
You can stay here for the time being.

The apartment was owned
by an aunt of his
who was off on a world tour.

So we got to live there
absolutely free.

Furnished
really posh
in the middle of the city.

Sometime later a telegram came saying
she was on her way home.

Uncle Tryggve just said
Don't worry Mrs Fóth
we can sort this out.

I'll come at five o'clock again.

He picked us up in the BMW
and drove out to Solbacken
a really nice residential area in Malmö.

He pulled in
outside a detached three-storey house
and said you can live here.

There are two conditions
though, he said.

The first was
that his aunt living in Amiralsgatan
could move in on the ground floor
since she no longer wanted to live right in the city

The second thing was
we would take in a boy
from another Hungarian family
and treat him as one of our own.

That's where we lived for fifteen years or so.

For a tiny rent.

He said
We've bought this building
as an investment.

Though it was pretty clear
he was doing it for us.

448 | *István Fóth b. 1943*

My older sister Sussie
and Mum
got jobs in the factory.

My younger sister Katti . . .
she was sent to a girls' school.

As for me . . . I was sent away.

I wasn't allowed to stay
with my own family
instead I had to live with their family in Örkelljunga
with one of his brothers
in order to learn Swedish.

I had been in Year Seven at school in Hungary.

They put me back two classes
and I went into Year Five.

That was really good
as I was able to get into the language.

I went to art college
Konstfack in Stockholm
to study decorative painting
and public environment.

I learned a lot at that college.

Nice college.

Still a popular course of study.

But it's a course that pretty well
guarantees you'll be unemployed.

This was during the nineteen sixties
and the ethos of the college was free and open.

Challenging . . . almost provocative you might say.

Come on . . . be demanding
for fuck's sake.

That sort of thing.

I tend to think of it
as being an upbringing
as much as an education.

While I was still in my last year
at art college
an artist from Denmark arrived.

He was called Palle.

He said we were going to create an exhibition . . .
he called it
Model for a Qualitative Society.

It was to be put on
at the Museum of Modern Art in Stockholm
and he needed a gang
of about twenty art students.

We removed all the paintings
covered all the floors
emptied the place completely.

Then we travelled round the country
begging materials.

Building materials
theatre costumes
paint.

We had great heaps of all kinds of things
and then we opened the doors to kids.

I think twenty-four thousand
kids came in a fortnight.

All they wanted to do was make things . . . endlessly.

Our job was to help them.

Not direct them but help them.

When parents came in and saw this
while dropping off their children
their first reaction wasn't
Wow
How fantastic!

But
Is this really allowed?

The presence of parents
inhibited the children so much
that we opened a café.

We moved the parents away to a separate space
and provided TV coverage of the main hall
so they could watch their children on TV.

Pär Stolpe who was a boss at the museum
won the commission
to create something to be called the Sweden House.

It's in Kungsträdgården park.

It was to be the public face of the Swedish Institute.

The opening was planned as a great splash
with a super exhibition.

Pär needed assistance
so I pitched in
and did all the décor.

The motto of the exhibition was
Sweden Today.

The aim was to give people a sense
of their place in existence
and Sweden's in the world.

The exhibition was incredibly modern.

Don't forget this was sixty-eight
and there were hardly any computers
but we had one.

It was a sort of box.

You could go up to it
and press a button
and up would pop
Hello
What's your name?

It was really out-of-this-world.

Then it would ask what you were called
and how you were doing.

Then came the question
What did you have for breakfast?

You entered all that
and this mannikin answered
OK István
I can inform you
that you have consumed this number of calories
and this much protein
and just for comparison
people in India consumed so-and-so much
and people in China so-and-so much.

We also had two TV crews
whose job was to produce reports
on current events in Sweden
and come back in the evening and show them.

There weren't any big screens in those days
but we had a rear projector
which projected an image from behind
making it look like a big screen.

The Swedish Institute
was really looking forward to this
and laid on a full-scale run-through
but all hell broke loose
I can tell you.

They'd assumed
it would show pretty pictures
of red cottages with white corners
and the Swedish flag.

It was supposed to be lakes and beauty
that being what Sweden was.

But this bloody T V crew
had found a place
where a wifey in Stockholm
had crammed fifteen Turks into one room
and fleeced every one of them for rent.

That was a sort of Sweden too!

458 | *István Fóth b. 1943*

What they said then was you can show anything
and open the exhibition
but on the sole condition
that the Swedish Institute is allowed
to censor all the material.

That's not the kind of thing you say to Pär.

All hell broke out.

It ended in conflict.

With us simply occupying
the whole of Sweden House.

And with large-scale demonstrations
in Kungsträdgården Park.

Have you heard of Siri Derkert?

She'd created a large wall sculpture.

It was due to be unveiled
to coincide with the opening of the exhibition.

But she refused.

She said
I'm not going to unveil it
until the exhibition opens.

What is it they're showing
that's so utterly awful
that it mustn't be exhibited?

I don't remember what the solution was.

In any case there wasn't an exhibition.

Pär wouldn't go along with being censored.

There were hard men
on both sides.

Many people came out in Kungsträdgården
and it was during that time that . . .

Many of us were like-minded.

We were working in sizeable groups
and a lot of the people in these groups were discussing
the idea that maybe we didn't have to be crammed into the city
but should give some thought
to moving out to the countryside
and living and working there instead.

Then along came the next trend
the green wave.

Eating loads of vegetables and the like.

But that wasn't us.

I moved out in sixty-nine
up to Sysslebäck.

We didn't share the vision
of becoming farmers in the countryside.

That wasn't the sort of society
we had in mind at all.

What we had instead
was a genuine work collective.

We started off in factories and industries.

That's something the green wave never did.

The idea of moving up here . . .
it was partly because this is where
you can get hold of
the raw material, wood.

Given that I had plans
to make a lot of wooden playpark equipment
it seemed logical
to work in an area
where there was plenty of the raw material
for what I was going to do.

Things didn't work out well up in Sysslebäck.

Then I found this place.

It was a forest plot.

The house itself was falling down at the time.

Hardly any of it was standing upright.

Bôlla, Ingeborg
was keen to sell it to me
but I wasn't allowed to buy it.

At that time you had to be
either a neighbour or a farmer's son
to be allowed to buy forest or land.

Folke Ekberg
who was a practical man and good with finance
said
István, this is what you have to do . . .
Bôlla, Ingeborg, sells the whole lot
to the Board of Agriculture.

The Board of Agriculture splits it
so that you get to buy the house and
the plot you want
as well as a bit of land
and I'll buy the rest
that's what Ekberg said.

It was a good deal for him
and that was how I was able to buy
one part of the divided farm.

I didn't become a Swedish citizen
until I was twenty-seven.

It took a hell of a long time.

It meant I wasn't called up
for military service
when I was eighteen . . .
I was attending art college
or had just finished there
when I was first called up.

By that stage I'd done some thinking about existence.

And then there's the fact that our history
during the Second World War
was pretty dramatic.

It's actually a miracle
I'm sitting here now.

When I was called up I said
I don't think this is going to work out.

I don't believe in it.

I'd rather do civilian service.

I want nothing to do with weapons.

Their response was
In terms of your conscience
there is nothing to prevent you from doing armed service.

So I spent sixteen days
in the armed forces.

After just three days they sent for me
and said
You're not permitted to discuss politics
and make propaganda.

It's completely forbidden.

Aha
I said.

After a couple more days
they separated me from the group.

I was to sit in a room
and draw maps.

We were still able to meet and discuss things
in the evenings.

They were cheerful lads
they'd just been issued with their shooters
but I saw things from a different point of view.

They threw me out
after sixteen days
and I was sent to gaol instead.

I was kept in for a month the first time.

Then a year or two later
they re-called me
and asked
What's your attitude to military service now?

Just the same as before.

I don't want anything to do with it.

OK . . . in that case it'll be two months.

Consequently when the entry date
for this property arrived
I was still inside.

I came here two weeks later.

I went up to Sysslebäck first
and picked up Ulla and Johan
my son.

Then we drove down here in our old VW.

When we got to the farm
the house was packed
absolutely full of people.

The jungle drums had been beating in Stockholm
István has bought a farm in Värmland
Let's go!

That's how our commune started.

We hadn't really planned it
it just happened.

From when we started in nineteen seventy
up to seventy-six . . .
just six years
but in those six years I think
something like three or four thousand people
passed through
for shorter or longer periods.

Word spread and became known
within certain circles
and people came.

We had many discussions.

On one occasion we invited people . . .
from eight different countries, I think.

We held a meeting
and discussed the problems of sparsely populated areas
in different parts of the world.

We had a minor problem of sorts
with regard to our neighbours
but somehow or other I discovered
there was demand for a course in batik work.

Enough people signed up for it
but there wasn't a course leader
capable of running it.

So I thought
Well what about it?

After all
art school is art school.

I've never done batik work of any size
but it surely can't be
that damn special.

So we took it on.

We turned the upstairs floor
into a large studio
and suddenly it became acceptable
for people to come to our place.

Twenty women from the local area
came every week
and enjoyed it.

The course finished
with all of us doing a piece of work together.

We made an enormous picture
bigger than the whole of this table.

In wax batik.

With the church in the middle
and sheep
and the landscape . . .
the whole of Stöllet in fact.

And everyone's name along the borders of the long sides.

We had it up in the stairwell.

When the commune broke up
I didn't feel
I had the right to keep it.

I took it to the church
and said
Can you look after this?

Local people made it
along with us.

We think it's a fine document.

It was good.

It was beautiful.

It made an enormous difference for us.

People could see now we weren't so dangerous.

Before then rumour had had it
that we did all the things
that people believed went on
in communes.

Taking drugs
having group sex . . .
you know
the sort of thing people were sure
communes got up to.

But after that things changed . . .
they said we didn't even drink a bottle of beer.

Our commune . . .
it could be hard work
but it could also be completely wonderful.

It took up six years of my life
that I wouldn't want to have missed.

This kind of commune
is like a mirror
of our society at large.

All the problems you find out there in society
you also get in this small society.

We had a vision
that everything should be judged
what we do
what we think
what we create
from a socialist perspective.

Until we found
what kind of thing socialism actually was . . .
it could be anything and everything.

From the most conscious clear-sighted Marxism
down to not making the beds
or cleaning your teeth.

Just as in society at large
there are always people
who pull their weight and do their best.

Who do the organising.

And there are always followers
who prefer to do as little as possible
but still want to be involved.

It's the same everywhere.

And you learn some truths
that hold equally true in the outside world . . .
it takes many people pulling in the same direction
to make things go well
but it only takes a few
pulling in different directions
for everything to go to hell.

We kept careful accounts.

Every krona we spent
was noted.

We shared the work.

Every day two people were picked out
to take care of the day's meals.

It never caused any problems.

We worked hard
and conditions were rough.

Basically we were living on top of one another.

But we could manage on sixteen kronor a day
per person.

Things were tough
but there weren't any disagreements.

But times changed.

We started manufacturing playpark equipment
and money began coming in.

Our economy was communal
so even though the ideas were mine
I didn't get more than anyone else.

It all went into a communal pot.

Then all of a sudden it became obvious
that we were taking in so much money
we could afford a hundred kronor
per person
rather than sixteen.

Our economy had grown that much.

That's when the problems started.

That's when the commune split
into two factions.

The commune now had two chiefs
each with his own vision.

I thought
Now things are going better
and we want to show it's possible to live
communally like us
I think we should use the money
to improve our living conditions.

Maybe each of us
could have a room of our own.

We could raise our standards.

Maybe spend some money on the house.

The other faction thought
that was a bad idea
and we'd promote our ideas better
by continuing to live on sixteen kronor
but with four times as many people.

There was no solution to this
and a large section of the commune moved
down to Hallandsåsen
and opened a new place.

And my family was left
in the house up here.

It was Jon Halvardsson
who built Nystugan.

The farm itself is old.

Goes back to the sixteen hundreds.

The farmhouse itself was over in the other direction.

It's gone now.

He built this place in nineteen hundred and seven
on a Norwegian design.

He wasn't short of money.

How did he lose it all?

He's said to have been very careful
about his choice of friends . . . later!

You know where our stable is?

Straight across the road from it
there's a small wooden building.

That's an old stable too.

That's where he ended up spending
forty years of his life
looking across at this place.

What a bloody awful fate!

I keep that story in mind.

I thought to myself
that if things go so badly
that I end up living in a stable
I'd better do up the stable.

So I did up the stable
and that's where I ended up.

The family grew apart.

And I moved out to the stable.

While I was in prison
I started designing playgrounds.

I got in contact
with a company called Brio.

We opened a workshop out here
and the commune made a good living from it.

We made something we called Finnskoga Play.

It came to be very well-known in Sweden
and down in Europe too.

What they called a playground before that
was no more than a sand pit
with maybe a swing and a roundabout.

We brought all the play elements together.

It was a complete play set-up
integrating all the functions of play.

Every playground looks like that these days
but we were the first to do it.

I worked with Brio for seventeen years.

After that I became more interested in water.

The company's called Recrea.

When I came up with things like this in the eighties
no one had been thinking along these lines.

What passed as water play at that time
was an arrangement of
pinnacles and towers and slides.

But we made something that's so simple . . .
a thing like this
full of life.

It's a slide
it's physical play
it's climbing.

We call them Bubbles.

Wet Bubbles.

We have a large workshop
so we can do all necessary work
with the fabric.

Print it
coat it
weld it.

The fabric part
is the major part in our products.

My dream is
to try to entice my son Johan
to come back home.

I'm an incomer
and I don't really feel
I'm an Oseboler.

It takes several generations
to become a native.

For the others I'm still a bit neutral.

It's OK if it's just me knocking on the door.

People visit people at home
but certain people
only visit certain people
not others.

If I invite a particular person
someone else won't come.

People are different.

Not everyone
gets along with everyone else.

It could result from something
that's been in the family for generations.

You just don't know.

If there was somewhere neutral
a neutral meeting place
it would be possible to cross these boundaries.

But there isn't anywhere of that kind.

I've got used to having space.

Both inside and out.

Freedom
and space
and then people . . .

In a place like this you don't have people around you
you have individuals.

You get closer to one another.

Törnsgårn is the old family home
built in eighteen forty-eight.

It was Grandad's parents' home.

He passed away in two thousand and three.

The house
was too much for Grandma after that.

I was interested in moving here.

In my job it makes no great difference
where I live.

I work at Skanska as a joiner.

Some of the time I'm at home
some of the time in Karlstad
and some of the time somewhere else.

There were three of them.

There was grandfather
Ture.

There was Anna-Karin's father
Henry.

And then there was Dagny.

This is where they came from.

Henry lived in that house there.

And Dagny took a house over in Stöllet.

This place was just standing here.

Axel was the last one to live in it.

Grandad's uncle.

He died in eighty-four
and it was pretty dilapidated even then.

They started renovating it in ninety-four.

Everything on the bottom floor has been replaced.

The upstairs
is as it was before.

I've tried to preserve it
with old floors.

Outside is as it was.

Except that up to ninety-four
the whole house was grey.

No colour at all.

I was always over with Gudrun
Anna-Karin's mother.

I went there
instead of going to a nursery
or the kinds of place they have these days.

That's where I grew up
if I can put it like that.

Many people replace things
when they own an old house.

They install geo-thermal heating
and don't use the wood burner.

But an old building works on the principle
of accepting draughts
and a ventilation system . . .
and then you go and remove it.

You get something that cools things instead.

You don't heat up the air that circulates.

A host of things goes wrong then.

I think it's cosy
when the fire's burning.

That's the coffee machine
spluttering and plopping now.

But I've actually lighted
a fire today.

It was a bit chilly
this morning.

Christer Larsson b. 1982 | *497*

You go and buy timber for
a new house these days.

The kind of timber you get
wouldn't have been used for firewood
in the twentieth century.

They simply don't care.

They just sell it
and the people buying it have no idea
what it ought to be like.

A plank for instance.

These days they want to get things done
as fast as possible
and get paid.

It used to be OK to take longer.

They selected the trees they were going to use
for panelling for example.

They would take them from a place
where they knew growth had been slow
and the timber was good and hard.

There isn't anyone these days who . . .
they don't even know which way round
to face a plank
when they're putting it in.

Christer Larsson b. 1982 | 499

We've been considering
building a veranda on the back.

Something in the old style.

Trying to preserve
something of what used to be.

At the same time it'll have to be practical
if we're going to be able to use it.

But I don't want to just
stick on something hyper-modern
something that looks . . .
well, twenty ten
on an old nineteenth century house.

I grew up in Ambjörby.

There's a little house in the forest
away to the left
by the football field
it can't be seen from any direction.

This is downtown
compared to that.

You can see loads of houses all round here.

It's nice to go into town
now and again.

But when I've been there a day
I want to get home.

It's calm and peaceful.

I go out and do
pretty well what I like
in my own little world.

No doubt some people panic
or feel isolated
but I feel at peace with it.

There are days
when there's nothing to do
it's boring
but it's just a matter of using your imagination
or taking it as it comes.

I used to take part in rallies.

My father didn't like it at all.

The rally car I drove
had things
that recorded top speeds.

It was a big mistake
for him to learn about that computer.

When I came in for servicing
the first thing he'd do
wasn't to change the tyres
but to press that thing.

Then he'd just yell at me.

Hundred and seven miles an hour
on that section!

It was a narrow gravel road
with loads of trees.

You don't think about it when you're driving.

So I put it out of mind.

Christer Larsson b. 1982 | *503*

I was interested
in riding motocross
and lived in a suitable place
to do it without disturbing anyone.

Out in the forest.

Where there's no one who'll have heard
or seen anything.

Then later on I saw the bigger boys
driving on frozen lakes in winter
in ordinary cars.

It looked cool.

If something breaks
you have to repair it.

If you can't
you have to give it a go
or ask someone else who can
and that way you learn.

I've done a bit of stock car racing occasionally
just to have taken part.

We have a race in Höljes next weekend.

There are three hundred entries in my class.

It's one of the biggest stock car races in Sweden.

Six cars line up and wait.

Then the red light changes
to green.

They set off all at once.

The first thing
is to survive the first corner.

I don't have a special tactic
for doing that.

But what matters is
to be well out in front.

That's half the battle.

Surviving the first corner.

You have to have
extremely quick reactions.

That's number one.

Then you have to have the right tyres on the car
so you can start as quickly as possible
and accelerate as quickly as possible
without skidding too much
or too little.

You have to have a good car.

If you're driving a bad car
what you do at the start
makes no difference.

Sometimes you think too much
and sometimes too little.

There's an enormous difference
between one situation and another.

You don't have many milliseconds
to decide whether to brake
or to put your foot down.

One or the other.

Christer Larsson b. 1982 | 507

Everyone wants to go through the first corner at the same time
and for instance in Höljes
there are three hundred of us.

Each of us drives four heats.

Unless you come first
in every heat
you won't be driving in Sunday's A-final.

A second place is not enough.

So it's quite . . .

No one gives anything away willingly
if I can put it like that.

I take part in elk hunts.

But I'm not fanatical about it.

I go along mainly
because I think it's good company.

We have a get-together in the middle of the day
and in the morning.

If it wasn't for that
I'd never think of taking part.

I own forest land and hunting rights
and have been taking part since I was small
so it was the natural thing to do.

But there's a bit of a difference between
now and when I first took part.

There are just twelve or fifteen of us today.

The first time I took part
there were fifty of us.

Not having a dog
that I let out in the forest
I don't have any trouble with wolves.

We shouldn't be blaming them for everything.

It's down to the hunters too.

There can be no doubt that there are fewer elk
now than there used to be.

You can't compare it with the eighties.

But they aren't as bloody rare
as people like to make out.

In our case finding the elk
isn't the problem.

We don't have enough people.

That's the problem.

There are such big gaps
that they can slip through anywhere.

It's absolutely bloody obvious
that wolves take elk.

We've got plenty of wolves.

You can see that when there's snow in winter . . .
loads of tracks.

We've had the odd solitary wolf
passing Nystugan.

But we take the horses in at night.

Though I don't think a wolf would go for horses.

There'd need to be more than one of them.

But it's not very pleasant
knowing they might be round the corner.

We've got a bear too
roaming around the district
that's been here for at least ten years.

A single one
which hangs out between Ruskåsen and Osebol shieling.

No doubt he takes the occasional elk.

It's all part of nature
so it's obvious wolves should exist.

But we don't need to have
as many as we have these days.

Especially not in such a small area.

They should be spread out
across the whole of Sweden.

As soon as a wolf appears
anywhere near a town
it's seen as a catastrophe.

But out here
where we have heaven knows how many of them
it's unimportant.

Attitudes are a bit different.

Everything should exist
as long as there isn't anything
anywhere near a town.

I've often wondered
about that bridge.

Let's hope they find they've got
too much money in some heritage fund
and realise
it's the only two-arch bridge
still left.

There are lots
with only one arch
but this one is double.

I think something will be done
quite soon.

A lot of stonework and bits are falling off.

Demolition presumably.

Even if that ends up costing
X million
it's probably only half
what it would cost to renovate it.

What I'd miss most
if they took it down
is the ability
to walk across to the other side.

Taking a morning walk
or an afternoon walk
in the sun.

I've got one of those old wheels out there
the sort used for the old ferry
which used to be winched across.

It was lying down there by the river
but it's out here now.

There's always been a crossing point here.

Obviously I want it to be kept.

Getting rid of things is just about the worst thing.

Things that have been kept for two hundred years
in case they come in handy.

God, the lorryloads of junk
we've driven away.

Everything from harnesses for horses
to a sort of potato grate
to furniture . . . everything.

Everything from real junk
to things that shouldn't really be thrown away.

Newspapers, glass bottles.

A mobile museum
combined with a recycling centre.

A town can't function without the countryside.

Take food for instance.

Everything from potatoes to vegetables to meat.

They're not produced in the town.

But out in the countryside.

So someone has to live out in the country.

A lot of knowledge is disappearing.

You've got people living in the countryside
who soon won't know how to grow potatoes.

There's not the same need
when you can buy them for next to nothing.

I've got someone leasing my land.

It's been put down to grass the last two years . . .
it's for his animals.

For hay and silage.

It's good someone is cultivating it
so it doesn't get overgrown.

There used to be potatoes all the way
from here down to there.

Now I just plant up one of those little growboxes
and it gives us potatoes for half the winter.

We still do it
but just for our own use.

We don't get through that many potatoes.

It used to be potatoes every day.

Now it's more often pasta.

When we lived in Trollhättan
every evening when Dad came home
he'd listen to the radio
after we'd finished eating.

He used to lie down on the floor
in a particular place
below that radio
and I'd be there as well
making a fuss.

So I know
when war broke out
we heard it on the radio.

Mum came from Östmark.

The reason we moved there
was that Mum's parents
had a guesthouse and a shop.

It was an uncle of mine who ran the shop
until he was called up.

And then . . .
the only one able to move
was Mum.

Dad must have been called up too
but he was working for Saab Aero Engines
at the time.

We had loads of refugees coming over
from Norway.

They'd come across the frontier
then move down in the Östmark direction.

We could hear when bombing was going on.

You could hear there was war.

It was more than twenty miles but you could still hear it.

I wasn't very big
but I remember it.

They were frightened
and were short of clothes to wear.

It was winter and cold.

Mum and Grandad
collected what they could get hold of.

There were many soldiers in Östmark.

They closed the guesthouse
and had an officers' mess
and rooms for visitors upstairs.

And I know they had . . .
they were in clink.

If it was the lower ranks
who'd done something . . .
they were locked up there for a couple of days
and food was taken up to them.

I was so happy on Thursdays
when I got pea soup.

I would join in fetching the food.

They picked it up at the field kitchen.

But the officers didn't eat there
they had a table to sit at, them.

I was only there
because I got pea soup from them
and a pancake.

I don't remember being afraid exactly
but I did feel sorry for them.

The ones who came here . . .
the refugees.

I felt sorry for the soldiers too.

They had to walk from Torsby
it was slushy
and they got soaked
and they hadn't been fed.

It's a good twelve miles.

They were soaked through when they arrived.

But you know
what happens is one thing
and how you perceive it another.

Something that's worked really well
for our folk history society
is baking flatbreads
which we make on slabs
heated on the spot
at markets and so on.

That's earned some money.

There are a lot of buildings
in the folk museum
and old bits and pieces have been donated.

But it has to be kept organised.

And someone has to do it.

People don't need societies these days.

A rheumatics association
or supporting research
that can be nice enough.

But otherwise . . .

You have a car
and you can go wherever you like.

Press a button on the TV
and you've got home entertainment.

People used to get together in their homes
and chat.

Now you have to be invited before you go.

People are mobile in a different way.

And you have the telephone.

Not many people had
telephones in those days.

People don't stay home with their children
like they used to.

I find it hard to believe
it's better for them
to be put in a nursery
than stay at home.

I'm not denying
that it's good there is one.

But just think what it's like living here
and wanting a job at the hospital
starting at seven.

You have to drop the child off at six.

Which means you get the wee one up at five.

I feel sorry for them
and not just for the children.

It's a pity for the parents
living with that kind of pressure.

I'll tell you something.

Everyone in our house was always busy
but there was always someone available.

If it wasn't Mum or Dad
there was Granny, Grandpa, Uncle Axel . . .
always someone.

On the other hand none of them
had time to sit down
and knit a pair of stockings.

We got them from the shop.

All the other children's
were handknitted.

That made me so miserable.

One day a woman asked Mum
what was upsetting me.

Because she hasn't got handknitted stockings
she said.

If you've got some wool
I can take it home with me
and knit the lass a pair of stockings.

I was over the moon
when I got those stockings.

But it didn't last more than a day.

They were so itchy
they nearly drove me mad.

The ones they got from the shop
were so nice and soft.

It wasn't the same wool.

This was real wool you know.

The others brought their own food to school
so they wore pinafores
which I never did.

I lived no farther away from the school
than the distance over to Alvar's place
so Mum thought
I should come home to eat instead.

All the others wore pinafores, they did
presumably because they spilt food and made a mess.

So I said to Grandma
Can't you make me a pinnie?

As luck would have it
school photos were being taken the following day.

I've got a photo
where I've pushed myself to the front
and I do believe I'm the only one
wearing a pinafore.

I was so happy.

All kinds of things can make you happy!

When Ture passed away
István came and said
Why are you still pottering about here
when I've got a first-rate flat up there
standing empty.

Have you
I said.

I'll come up with you and have a look.

Christer was old enough
to be thinking about
moving away from Mum and Dad.

I realised it was too much for me
that house was
and it needed things doing to it.

So he took it over
and I don't regret it for a moment.

Ture felt more at home here I think.

The fact he could go out
and do things whenever he wanted.

It's not like that in a flat.

We lived on the second floor
and there were stairs.

We used to drive down to Karlstad now and again
but come the end he just wanted to be here.

He was like Axel.

He used to light the stove in the kitchen.

It gave him something to potter about with
and then he'd go in and have a lie down.

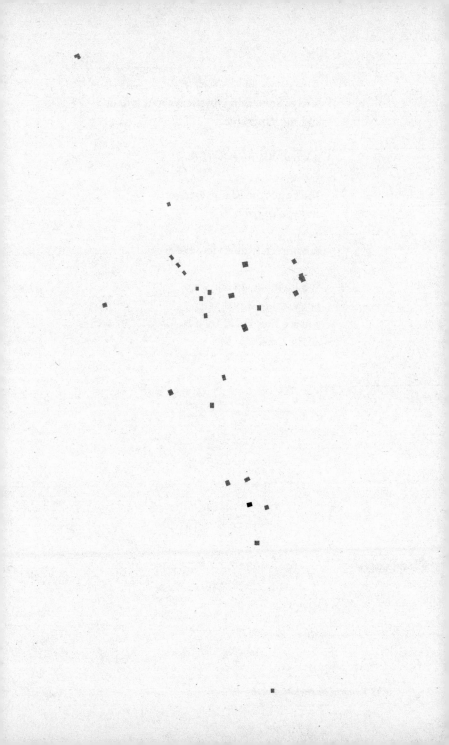

There's something mystical about it here
and so changeable.

It looks different every day.

You've got the Klarälven river
and you've got hills.

A completely new view every day.

Whether you go one way
or the other way
you see how beautiful it is
all the time.

The fact that it's harsh here
and rugged
I find that attractive.

I want it to be rugged.

I want raw nature.

If you're afraid of that
you shouldn't be here.

It's a survival thing.

That's probably why we both like it.

What we want is . . .
you have to get by.

You have to survive
and get by, whatever happens.

My favourite place
is the heart attack path.

You walk up behind the house here.

It was the first thing I did
when I moved here.

I wanted to explore
the forest around me.

I have to get out into the forest
otherwise I go crazy.

I walk up to a viewpoint.

There's a rock there
I sit on
and give my dog Grace
a biscuit.

I've been there in all kinds of situations.

When I'm in a good mood.

When I'm angry.

When I'm sad and weepy.

When I've been really ill.

I want to look out over the whole valley.

The Klarälven river.

In the snow.

I've sat up there in the snow.

I grew up in Silicon Valley.

My parents came from Karlstad.

We used to come to Sweden for summer holidays.

The best time of my life
was when I was a child with my cousins and friends
in the house by Lake Gapern.

We played with pigs
and swam in the lake
and went fishing.

That's why I moved to Sweden.

I wanted forests.

A new direction in life.

My parents had moved back to Sweden.

I followed five years later.

They helped me get started.

But getting a job here is difficult.

Especially for an American.

No one here takes an American seriously.

They think we're a shower of idiots.

I've worked a lot in the care sector
in the USA too.

I like the social part of it.

Visiting old people in their homes
and hearing their stories
of what things used to be like.

They offer you coffee sometimes
if you have time.

Sometimes you don't.

If you do, you sit with your coffee
and chat about anything and everything.

Sometimes it can get really intimate.

Tears or laughter.

Being appreciated
by someone who's all alone.

I've got grannies and grandads
all over the river valley.

They want to cut back by one firefighter per station.

At present there are three of us
for call out.

Five years ago
there were five.

That made things really safe.

Straight after that it went down to four
then to three.

Now they want to cut one more
so there'll only be two
to respond to call-outs.

It'll be impossible to do anything worthwhile.

You have to stop the traffic.

That's not easy
as drivers just don't understand.

I would reckon that almost everyone
has come close to being knocked down
at least once or more
at roadside call-outs.

People drive on past
even when there's a stop light.

They're in a hurry.

You can imagine
how many people would suffer
if an accident happened
and a firefighter was injured
or killed
during call-out
by a motorist ignoring
traffic conditions.

With only two firefighters on call
it just won't work.

We came to a decision.

Right, we've had enough.

We'll resign.

And we did.

Thirty-two of us in all.

But they've made us
take back our resignations.

We did it
to stop our union being sued.

They claimed it was a threat.

Industrial action
aimed at influencing local politicians
while they were planning
what to do in the future.

But we already know what the result will be.

Everyone counts on us turning out.

Everyone knows everyone else out here.

We have local knowledge.

Everyone feels safe because we're here
but that feeling of security
is starting to disappear.

No one knows
what the future will be like.

If they do shut down
the emergency service in Stöllet
it might well lead to the closure
of other things.

The simple fact is that people will move away.

Cut the services
and people won't want to live here.

Ingrid Sarnefors b. 1965 | *549*

I've been here a couple of years.

I want to do my bit for the community.

There's not much I'm frightened of.

I'm fairly strong
and have a lot of outdoor experience.

It teaches you discipline
and how to look after yourself
and be self-reliant.

I'm also really nosy.

I like doing physical work
and to feel I've done a good job
and helped people.

And having colleagues
is really great.

Firefighters are special people.

They're laid-back.

They're down-to-earth
because they've been through a lot
and seen a great deal.

They view humanity in a different way.

I don't think I'm a hero
but I see the others as being so
and I think it's great to be part
of that environment.

I've attended traffic accidents.

There've been grassland fires
and forest fires
and house fires.

Waiting for an ambulance to arrive.

Someone's taken ill at home
or out in the forest.

All kinds of things can happen.

Trees get blown down
and have to be cleared away
and cut up.

When you're on an emergency call-out
if it's something serious
we have silly conversations
and laugh
on our way there.

As we approach the scene of the accident
and the radio tells us the situation
the car goes quiet.

People prepare themselves
for the worst that can happen.

Everything goes quiet.

On the way back from an emergency
we have a debriefing in the car.

We talk among ourselves
about what happened.

You can say anything at all.

No one is judged for how and what they feel
after going through something dreadful.

When we get back to the station
we have another debriefing
with Stefan
our head of station.

We usually do it as a group
and you can have a private conversation afterwards.

You might go and sit in the fire engine
close the door
so no one can hear you.

You can cry or do whatever you need to in there.

Keeping things the way they are now
that's all we want.

We're not demanding
loads of money.

We just want things to stay as they are now.

The level of manning we have at present
and the possibility of appointing more
and getting the training we need.

Sweden has lots of natural wilderness.

The Netherlands
is nothing but towns.

No real forests at all.

The Netherlands is
twice the size of Värmland.

Seventeen million people live there.

The sparsely populated areas of Sweden are enormous
but the number of people living there
is getting smaller and smaller.

There aren't any young people left.

They all move to large cities
and don't grow up in the forests any longer.

Many Swedes
have lost contact with nature.

Survival
walking in the forest . . .
they just aren't used to it.

They only recognise chanterelles
and porcini.

There are many other mushrooms
that are good
much better in fact
but people don't know them.

We started beaver safaris in Ekshärad.

It was going well
but after three or four years
they shot all the beavers
and cleared the trees
because the local people wanted to go fishing.

So we moved to another place
by Björbysätern.

It was good
better than Ekshärad in fact.

A beautiful area
out in the wilds.

People liked it
and we always saw beavers.

We had flooding last year.

The beavers moved out of their lodges.

Many of them were attacked by wolves.

It made them nervous, anxious.

They didn't show themselves any more.

As soon as they saw us . . . plop.

We stopped doing beaver safaris.

There was no point.

For my part I actually like wolves.

They need to find their place again
among us
but they are too concentrated.

And it's not really possible
to move wolves.

They have territories.

They stick to them.

All animals have a right
to a place in the natural world.

If I earn less money as a result
I'm not going to starve.

Many people think differently though.

They're filled with hate.

They think of wolves as terrible monsters.

That's what they think.

We all have to eat.

Bushcraft did well last summer.

Interested tourists
get the chance to come out
and read nature.

Navigate without maps
without a compass
without GPS.

How to find your way
out of the forest
if you get lost.

How to locate
north, south
east and west.

Even in the dark
without stars.

We light fires
and they cook their own food.

They build shelters
where they can spend the night.

I used to do this for the armed forces.

I was an instructor
in sports, climbing
and survival.

I was doing that for thirty-two years.

It's really good for civilians too.

A little bit different
compared with the forces
but essentially the same thing.

I'm a marine commando.

We're specially trained
for anti-terror operations
climbing, abseiling
diving, sharpshooting.

At the start of training there are
two hundred, two hundred and fifty men selected.

By the end only twenty to thirty are left.

Four weeks before the end of training
I was run down by a moped
and fell on my weapon.

I lost a number of teeth
and my jaw was broken.

They expected me to drop out
but I didn't want to.

That was in seventy-eight
when we had a horrendously cold winter.

For the last four weeks
it stayed between fifteen and twenty-six below zero
in the Netherlands.

Every day involved a lot of running
and marching
and climbing hills.

I hardly had any food.

I started at ninety-three kilos.

When I finished I weighed sixty-eight.

I didn't have an easy time as a child.

I had to fight a lot.

I'll always be a fighter.

And I'm extremely stubborn.

Oh-oh!

That makes two of us.

We're exactly the same.

Geert Cornelis 'Geco' Denkers b. 1956
Ingrid Sarnefors b. 1965 | 567

My body's worn out now.

Problems with my back, my legs.

My knees are wrecked.

Overloading, overloading.

Too little rest.

Nothing but training, training, training.

Hillwalking with a forty-kilo pack.

It's great fun and no problem
when you're young
but not when you get older.

You're not up to it any longer.

The pension age for marines is fifty-three.

It's actually an early pension.

You get a military pension
until you reach the normal pension.

I was fifty.

I visited Norway for the first time
at the end of the seventies
start of the eighties.

I thought then
this is where I want to live
when I retire.

When I was close to pension age
I checked out Norway
but it was far too expensive.

So I thought
I'll check on Sweden.

It's much better here
than in Holland.

You have the natural world.

It's calm.

People aren't so aggressive.

There are too many people
in a small space down there.

Think of Malmö
think of Stockholm
think of Gothenburg.

The more people
and different people
that live in a small space
the more aggression you get.

Aggression and violence.

When they see you with a mobile
they want a mobile too.

You've worked to get it.

They don't have an income
so they steal it.

There are loads of situations
where people get aggressive.

I'm like that too
can't keep my mouth shut.

So it's just as well
I no longer live in Holland.

Or in the city.

You have to live even in the summer.

If you're working in outdoor activities
your whole time is taken up with tourists
and you can't do the things you want for yourself.

And Ingrid has a permanent job now.

      In the kitchen at Klarastrand old people's home.

         The great thing about outdoor activities
         is meeting so many different people.

         You become friends with some of them.

            The downside is
         that you meet too many different people.

            It takes a lot of energy.

         But however worn-out you feel
          you can go out into nature
            and regain your strength.

Geert Cornelis 'Geco' Denkers b. 1956
Ingrid Sarnefors b. 1965 | 571

We've been living here for five years now.

Swedes tend to keep themselves to themselves.

It's difficult to become part of the community.

It becomes easier and easier
after a few years.

They come to accept you bit by bit.

Last year an ex-colleague
bought a house in Stöpafors.

They live there all year.

Another colleague
came here on holiday for two summers
and looked at house after house.

They're going to move here too.

If you go round
believing you're somebody
that's how you'll be treated.

You should treat people
the way you want to be treated yourself.

You have to be careful
but if you show respect for others
you'll be treated the same way.

If you do something
and it's something useful
it will be appreciated.

That's how simple it is to live here.

That's what I think.

There were brothers and sisters
and neighbours' children.

We didn't make demands.

We'd be out in the sandpit
that used to be outside.

When we were children we took
the initiative much more
than our children do.

We've had this discussion
many times.

That there's nothing to do
and it's . . .

                                        What is there to do then?

What is there to do indeed?

That's just it.

Annica Barhammar b. 1976
576 | *Celina Barhammar b. 2002*

We were more creative
about finding things to do.

There weren't any electronic gadgets
when we were small.

I was quite old
when video came in.

Physical activities were what
occupied most of our time
I think that's much better
than the upbringing
children get these days.

Celina thinks
I'm unbelievably old-fashioned
when I talk like that.

Yes!

Annica Barhammar b. 1976
Celina Barhammar b. 2002 | 577

We used to play in the sand pit
that was out there.

We'd run at it from the south
and jump
and measure
who'd gone farthest into the pit.

Then you had to jump out
and do the same thing again.

That was our daily exercise.

Children ought to get more exercise, I think.

Like we did when we were younger.

Of course we fell over when out skiing
but that didn't mean you got a broken leg.

It seems to have to do with brittle bones.

I don't know how much scientific proof there is
but it seems to be a noticeable trend.

It takes a very great deal of force
to break strong bones.

Bone structure gets denser
if you hop and jump.

That's where the sandpit comes in.

They're going to expand the A&E department
so that's progress.

It's a sign they're putting money into it.

It removes the threat of closure
for the immediate future anyway.

Patient numbers are increasing.

There's more pressure
in the winter season when Branäs is open
and the population of Torsby district
increases by ten thousand.

Mostly broken bones
or head injuries.

Every holiday
sees a huge increase in bones needing plastering.

It's pretty much
a conveyor belt.

I think the Likenäs health centre
will eventually end up in Branäs.

I think that's quite likely
given the numbers going skiing there.

We were wondering
whether to buy a house up there.

The rental possibilities are really good.

It's booked up the whole winter season.

Buying a house is an investment
but prices have gone up
so much that . . .

The one we went and looked at
was seventy-five square metres.

Built in ninety-one.

Nothing had been done to it.

It went for a million and a half.

                                    Thirty-two people at the viewing.

Going like a city up there!

Annica Barhammar b. 1976
582 | *Anders Barhammar b. 1972*

I grew up in Gravol.

Three miles south of here.

                                        A bit more surely.

Well, maybe four.

Not so far away.

It was a shorter drive
when the bridge was open.

Anders Barhammar b. 1972
Annica Barhammar b. 1976 | *583*

It was the campsite.

Björkebo Camping.

Granny and Grandpa started it.

There were always new people in the summer.

New friends.

There was a lot more activity then.

A lot of them were regular visitors
who came back year after year.

Germans and Dutch and Norwegians.

I used to work there when I was still at school.

Middle school and upper school.

Cutting the grass and dealing with the garbage and . . .
started driving early.

Drove round the roadways in an old Amazon.

Dad's careful about that sort of thing
but it worked all right then.

I was driving a car
on the campsite
when I was in Year Six or Seven.

Apart from that he was strictly law-abiding.

It was sold off two years ago.

Germans bought it.

They're a family too
so that's good.

Dad took it over at the start of the eighties.

Left his job at the telephone company
and worked there full time . . .
there and in the forest.

In one sense that was freedom
but there was never a holiday.

We always stayed home in the summer.

But it didn't bother us.

Close to the river
and fishing and swimming.

We were thinking of moving to Norway
before we bought this place.

Or I was thinking about it a bit . . .
me and the children.

But you said 'no way' straight out.

He's loyal to this district is Anders.

> We were in Karlstad staying with friends
> looking round and getting a feel.

> But there's more competition in a city.

> Here your name is known.

> You're familiar with everything.

> It's difficult to get a job in the city
> without a proper education.

> So here we are.

> And I think that's just fine.

Yes.

It was a good decision.

Annica Barhammar b. 1976
Anders Barhammar b. 1972 | *587*

I lived in Torsby in the nineties.

But I always longed to come back here.

I never really felt at home there.

I spent a lot of time in Gravol whenever I was free.

I've always been drawn
up here.

I was offered a job up in Likenäs.

It's good to be able to come home in the evenings.

Salesman is what the description said
but it's actually a bit of everything.

On the till, and sheet metal work, and sales
yes, anything to do with the building trade.

I enjoy it there.

It's grown.

That's another thing that's thanks to Branäs.

That's what keeps the store going.

Branäs provides work for you and for me.

Anders Barhammar b. 1972
Annica Barhammar b. 1976 | 589

And they're spending money on the cottages.

They keep their value
if they're properly looked after.

The best thing would be
for them to be made permanent
but at least they're doing them up
which means the buildings will last.

Which is a good thing, after all.

It's like another world up there.

                                                        Like a little city.

                                                      Apartment blocks.

You should go and have a look if you've got time.

You can't see much from the road.

You have to go up to the top.

                              It's a real mountain environment up there.

                                  Down in the valley it's just like here.

                                     The kids have season tickets.

                                They're there more or less every weekend
                                          both Saturday and Sunday.

We go there at the first sign of spring
once the sun . . .

We usually go away at Easter.

                                        Yes, in the spring
                                        to escape the cold.

Anders Barhammar b. 1972
Annica Barhammar b. 1976 | *591*

I don't think
very much has been said
about what keeps us here.

I don't know whether it's
because of growing up here . . .
which makes it more understandable
that you're going to like it here.

The question would maybe have come up more often
if you'd moved here from somewhere else.

Why did you end up here
up in the forest?

                                    For us it's more natural.

                                    This is where we belong in a way.

This house has a peculiar history.

It used to be in Ambjörby
in Månäs on the west side of the river.

They took down all the timbers.

Then Oskar up here
made a bundle of the lot
tipped it into the river
floated it down here
and pulled it out.

It was all separate logs.

Then they dragged it up here
and put it back together.

Oskar had a brother
who was a dentist.

He took it as a summer cottage.

He was a dentist
at the community surgery in Stöllet
but left there.

They fitted this place up
and he lived here
and had his practice out in the cabin.

We moved here in sixty-nine
just after he retired from dentistry.

There were still a few bits and pieces here.

His stuff was auctioned off
so his dentist's chair went to auction.

He was slightly . . .
he was rather given to drink towards the end
and then he had cataracts
so he wasn't exactly the ideal dentist.

We lived for a while in Ljusnäs.

But she already had a family before me.

I was living in Stöllet then.

Before living there
I'd lived for a time in Trollhättan
while he was working for Saab.

How long we were there?

Eighteen months I think.

It was going all right
I'd say
it was, kind of
but I moved back home anyway.

Lennart Olsson b. 1944
596 | *Siw Persson b. 1945*

I had a cottage
next to my parents' home in Ljusnäs
I still have it

It was a matter of building something there
if we were going to be able to stay there.

It wasn't exactly modern
if I can put it that way.

And then along came children and so on.

We wanted something better to live in.

There was nothing really that attracted me here
apart from the fact it was a house.

I stayed home with the kids
and then later on started work as a home help
then began working nights caring for the elderly
in Vitsand.

That's what I worked as until I stopped . . .
well, until my knee became too painful.

So I got a sick pension.

I was there many years.

And I enjoyed working there.

Working nights was good . . .
with only two of us on shift
we got to decide things for ourselves.

There was a lot of fuss and bother during the day
they were all enemies
and it wasn't good there in the daytime.

People didn't pull together.

Things worked well at night
because we always agreed
and could swap with each other
just as we liked.

And you do grow very close
when there's the just two of you working.

You get to know each other very well indeed.

We never had to say
Go and do this or that
because we knew what we had to do
and it worked.

Things have always worked out well
with people I've worked with.

It was much better
than being out doing home visits.

I like old people.

But if I've been visiting
one person, say
and then move on to the next
and they ask
How is she today?

I'm not allowed to say anything.

It can be difficult.

Everyone knows
something has happened next door
and that I've been there.

I may be really fond
of the person
but I still have to sit there and keep quiet
and say, well
I'm afraid I can't tell you.

Because you mustn't.

That's how it is.

I went fishing today
two bites . . . that's all.

Her name is Solveig
I do a lot of fishing with her
even in winter.

We fish out on the ice then
out on the Klarälv river.

In a bay . . . a sort of inlet.

We catch perch
which I give to her
as I don't eat it.

I don't like cleaning it
and dealing with it.

So she cooks it
and invites me to a meal.

I give any rainbow trout to her too.

It's a fish that's been introduced
and I don't want it.

I don't think it tastes good.

I don't know
but it just doesn't taste good.

I worked with Vänerskog
to the very last day.

The forestry combine
that went bankrupt in eighty-one.

It was Sweden's biggest bankruptcy.

Many forestry proprietors
lost a lot of money.

Enormous amounts.

It was an association of forest proprietors
but it grew a bit too big.

They bought up industries and . . .
well, it all came of over-optimistic forecasting.

After that it was all over in the forest
for a lot of people.

At the same time it marked a transition
from old-fashioned forestry
to a more modern sort
so it marked a huge change
in every way.

I started work in the forest
the day I was fourteen.

We were down here measuring timber.

We measured up everything prior to it being floated down.

It was the first job I had.

From the day of my fourteenth birthday.

Eighth of December nineteen fifty-eight.

We worked six days
because we worked half days on Saturday too.

Nowadays
they'd be charged with child labour.

But things were like that then.

You wanted to stand on your own two feet.

I was paid much worse but at least I got paid.

I bought a moped – cash down – in the spring.

It cost me eight hundred and forty kronor.

You had to measure the length and diameter
of every log they floated down-river.

So the buyer would know what he was buying.

It was floated down to Deje for sorting.

According to the markings
the timber would go where it was meant to go.

It had been measured up in the forest too
so they knew how much had been cut.

And they'd know roughly
what the difference was.

There was some theft
maybe not for firewood
but many people
well, maybe not that many
would help themselves and cut their own planks.

Not huge amounts
but it did happen.

And obviously
it had just happened to be floating past
as driftwood.

It was called the measurement association.

It was a grouping
of all the forestry companies.

The measurers who belonged to it
were on oath
so they were trusted absolutely.

Otherwise they'd have been able . . . well . . .
to pull their measurements out of a hat.

After all, it was the proprietor's capital
you were dealing with.

His assets anyway.

We were working along the Värån river and all round there
because in those days timber was even floated
down the tributaries of the Klarälv.

Measurements were taken during the winter
and on into spring.

After that I stayed in forestry work
right through to the eighties.

Every log had to be barked by hand
twigs taken off with an axe and a barking spade.

It was easy in the summer
but freezing in the winter.

It was pretty hellish.

It's impossible to describe
if you haven't done it yourself.

You had pains everywhere.

I have pains in my shoulders, that's for sure . . .
I think that's where it comes from.

Or maybe it's old age
but something's not right anyway.

At the start of the seventies
sixty-nine, seventy, or thereabouts
there was a revolution in forestry.

It happened little by little
but that's when it became noticeable.

That's when felling machinery came in
really modern machinery
by the standards of the day.

Things are so mechanised now
that there's scarcely a man
to be seen out there.

Many jobs just disappeared
which was maybe a good thing.

You have to keep up
with competition from the outside world.

You can't live in the past.

It's looks wonderful when you see
an old film of working with a horse in the snow
but you should know what really lay
behind that.

There was no factory work round here
not a thing.

And no tourist trade either
not in those days.

Many people moved away
and went to building work
in Stockholm and Gothenburg.

A lot of people found themselves working
away from home then.

You couldn't find work in Norway at the time
you had to go to the cities.

My hands got cut by the saw
twice
but the wounds healed up.

There were accidents, of course, but not . . .

The storm of sixty-nine
caused a lot to happen.

There were piles of storm-felled trees
and many amateurs
many forest proprietors
went into the forest.

For the most part they were the ones who got injured.

It's usually inexperienced people it happens to.

It was more or less like
it was with Cyclone Gudrun in Småland now.

Not quite so bad
but bad enough.

It was when we'd just moved here.

All Saints Day sixty-nine.

All the fallen trees.

It was unbelievable.

I don't think we'd been living here
more than a fortnight.

Mum and Dad had come
to visit and take a look
at the place where we were living
and then came this storm.

Trees were being blown down
when the time came to take them home.

I drove them home to Ransby.

They didn't have a car
so I fetched them and took them home.

Lennart Olsson b. 1944
Siw Persson b. 1945 | *611*

It was a couple of years later
that the bark beetle arrived.

Given the number of half-dead trees
the insects were able to thrive.

Traps worked
the principle was sound.

What attracts them
is pheromones
and they think there's a mate
in the trap.

There's a hole in the trap
well, a draining tube actually.

You put in a ribbon soaked in attractant.

They drop down into a container.

The principle worked
no doubt about that
but it was more or less like
peeing in the Atlantic Ocean
it had no effect at all
none.

We hunt
but our quota is very small now.

Not a tenth
of what it was at its height.

Wolves are part of it, but not all.

Hunters have culled too many
and it's possible there's less food
than there used to be.

There's not so much clear felling
for things to grow in.

There are various factors.

But wolves do have an effect
they do.

As things used to be
when elk were most numerous
there were actually too many of them.

Both for the environment
and the traffic
and everything else.

About half the number
would have been right.

But there ought to be
more than there are now . . .
maybe twice as many
at least.

We had permits for three elk last year.

The best we ever had was for thirty.

I've kept a photo from the eighties
when there were thirty-six of us out hunting.

Last year it was just fourteen.

Most of the missing numbers are outsiders.

But they're the ones who bring in the money
to rent the shooting and accommodation
and food and everything else.

So there's a loss of income
for local people
and landowners
and third parties involved in the hunt.

That's many, many millions
in Värmland alone.

I'm not one of those fanatics
but I can't be doing with wolves.

I wouldn't want to start a war
about wolves
I really wouldn't.

But there are some people who're completely . . .
it's worse than politics for some people.

Think of a Communist and a Sweden Democrat
that's what it's like with wolves.

Just last week I saw a wolf
down in Mjönäs.

It was lying in an outhouse
its leg was shattered up here.

How it got there
I don't know
whether it had been kicked by an elk
or knocked down by a car.

It had crawled in there.

The police came and collected it
so I've no doubt it's now in Uppsala
for a post mortem.

They've got the money for that.

If my summer cottage had been broken into
not a bloody soul would have come.

But they've got money for a wolf.

Värmlandsporten . . .
I worked there until I got my pension
plus two extra years
so I finished when I was sixty-seven.

I started there in January or February ninety-one
and was there virtually the whole time
both on the up and on the down.

It really was a dream.

It would have been interesting to see
what the commercial forecast was when it started.

Initially they had a gourmet restaurant there
two waitresses and a head-waiter every day.

And scarcely an eater in the place.

                    But it gave a lot of people jobs, anyway.

I stayed there through all three bankruptcies
but they take in a different sort of guest now.

If it hadn't been for the immigrants
it would have closed down by now
they provided a way to keep the restaurant going.

Lennart Olsson b. 1944
618 | *Siw Persson b. 1945*

When it started there were parties
Wednesday, Friday and Saturday.

A fair crowd of people
in its first and second year.

Then it was as always happens . . .
first the pleasure of novelty
and then it fizzles out.

There's nothing now.

I feel sorry for any youngster
growing up here these days.

Boys and girls stuck at home
never getting out.

They've got nowhere to go
to meet anyone.

Except for the Co-op
but there's no chance there . . .
if you're looking for a partner
there has to be some partying.

Lennart Olsson b. 1944
Siw Persson b. 1945 | *619*

The Branäs company bought
Ekebo Community Centre as a store.

The Branäs pub closes during the summer.

There are two or three events in Älgsjövallen Park
and one or two events a year
in Likenäs Park.

But to a great extent the place is dead.

                              The Dance Band Week in Malung.

This winter they tried things
in the Ambjörby Community Centre
but it was done on a voluntary basis

It wouldn't work
if they had to run it
with paid staff.

What made Värmlandsporten so good
was that many of the people came from elsewhere
so you got different company.

It's nice to see
people you've never seen before.

Lennart Olsson b. 1944
620 | *Siw Persson b. 1945*

We get a newsletter from the church.

I think there were three or four children
born last year
between Fastnäs and Långflon.

That shows you
the way things are going.

It shows you the facts.

If they go to school in Karlstad
they're likely to stay there.

They get used to living there.

There was a boy the same age as me
in the next village
so we hung around together.

For him and me it was quite natural
that a boy and a girl would play.

We used to cycle over to each other
and his dad's mum lived in Kårebol.

When he was visiting her
he'd come to my place
or I went there.

But in Stöllet . . .

Good god, do you hang around with a girl!

Well, that was news to him.

I was the only girl on the football team.

After three, four months
I realised for myself
that no, I'll drop out.

I realised that
as far as the trainers were concerned
it was only boys
who were supposed to be doing it.

But it was fun to give it a try.

Bored?
I was never bored.

You hear children these days . . .
God, how boring
God, how boring.

I never felt that.

I may have been isolated
and only had one friend
but there was so much to do.

I just wanted to join in
wanted to help out.

I was out in the summer
haymaking
and spring sowing
and learning to drive agricultural machinery.

I was never afraid.

The children say to me
Mum
you were living in the eighties
it's not like that today.

But we were never bored.

At the age of eleven or twelve
whenever I was told . . .
You must work hard at school
in order to get a good education.

You must take something
which you know will lead to a job.

I'd made up my mind even then.

I'm not going to move anywhere.

I'll stay here.

I saw the possibility
on the job front in Stöllet.

I thought
this is something they can't shut down
that quickly.

Most people take further courses and become
nurses and doctors and so on
but I feel I'm useful
doing what I do now
as a nursing assistant.

I've been working since I was seventeen.

Then I was pregnant with my son.

After that I got my first job working for the council.

At Klarastrand.

It's part of care for the elderly.

We've got sheltered housing too now.

For people who can't manage living in their own place
or want to move somewhere a bit more central.

It's like an ordinary flat
in Stöllet.

The difference is that you live
under the same roof as the staff.

The church choir comes to sing for them
on Sundays
and there's bingo and other activities.

That's where we come into the picture
as homecare staff
so that they get the help they need.

They may just want
to sit and talk and have
someone looking in on them.

We can see it's worth its weight in gold.

They're often just sitting there watching the clock.

Heavens, you're late
I thought something must have happened.

It's the highpoint of their day.

They're waiting for us to come.

I'm a nursing assistant
and I'm also a dementia support administrator.

Once the dementia nurse has made her assessment
she passes the information over
for us to follow up on it.

I have to see to it that the individual in question stays well.

It may be a case of
employing the right people.

It's important not to just take on anyone.

So many people nowadays
are afflicted in this way.

People used to shut their eyes to it.

That seems frightening to us now.

We were at a lecture
and I've heard people's stories about
how they used to lock them up in the old days.

It's a good thing we've moved on from that.

There's symptom relief and medication
that can slow the process down
and preserve their abilities.

I have many patients
all of them different.

Some of them want you to be serious.

Some of them want you to be jolly.

You have to adapt all the time.

In a way you learn to sense it.

Right, now we're off to the next one.

Right, this is the face we'll put on here.

And you just do it.

You play a part.

Like an actor all the time.

That's what it's like.

You don your mask
next patient
you don a new mask.

They're all different.

It's not like being in an office.

Old people give you so much in return.

Here comes the carer.

Goodness, how wonderful!

They would rather offer you coffee than be washed.

That's the little drop of life they really want.

Every day is different
even though we have the same patients
and the same staff.

It's a great bonus
for the people living here
not to have to deal with
a staffing agency that chops and changes
and sends twenty or thirty new staff.

People have it good here.

They know where they stand.

And it's good to be from around here yourself.

You know every single person.

Every single house.

Marie Björ b. 1983 | *637*

Our district runs all the way
from Likenäs down to Fastnäs.

Twenty-eight miles.

That means a lot of driving.

Many need several calls a day.

Three, maybe four a day.

You'll maybe drive
eighty, ninety miles
just around this area.

But those miles . . .

We think driving down to Karlstad
is wearing
but sitting in the car and driving round here
isn't wearing.

It's really rewarding
to get so much joy in return.

I've been doing this work
for many years now.

And I know how to organise things
to give me time for a cup of coffee with them
as well as doing whatever needs to be done.

I used to work in Stockholm
as a graffiti remover in the underground.

We worked with high-pressure hoses
and chemicals.

When I started there
we were using chemicals that weren't very healthy.

Towards the end of my time they changed over
to environmentally friendly substances.

But it turned into a real pain
because getting rid of the graffiti
became so difficult.

We used to paint on a chemical we called Dark.

It was coal-black
and it was caustic.

If I put a drop on my hand
and left it there
there'd be a flesh wound after a minute or so.

It was difficult to clean it off mexitiles.

They were white and very porous.

The graffiti soaked right in.

We had a high-pressure machine
and once when I was changing the nozzle
I was going to fit a nozzle
and was holding it like this . . .

And then . . .
whoosh . . . it went
and bugger me
it tore a piece of skin
right off my finger.

If I was working away at a tile
I might split it right across the middle.

We removed some good things.

There was a lot of rubbish too.

Places where they'd just taken a felt pen
and drawn a couple of strokes.

But there were others who used different colours
and put some time into it.

Shit, they were good.

Working nights at T-Centralen Station
was hell.

Trains came every three minutes or thereabouts.

I'd no sooner jumped down on the track
and started the machine
than a train came.

And youngsters playing silly buggers
would pull out the machine's plug.

You had to climb back up
and the track's a long way down.

One time I stayed down on the track.

He stopped the train
and shook his head.

It might have been an out-of-service train
that swished through non-stop.

I've worked in Norway on and off
doing joinery work.

We were in Oslo for a while.

The weeks were long.

Two hundred and fifty miles to drive home
and then leave again on Sunday.

Kevin was born at that time.

It was hard going.

But, but
it was well paid.

And that's what it's all about.

We were working for Skanska
but were just temporary.

It's like that these days.

Anyone who sets up a business
takes on temporary workers.

They can't employ me
and then have no work for me.

That would cost too much money.

Easier to take on temporary workers
and then sack them . . .
or not sack them.

We don't need your services any longer.

That's the way it works these days.

I chose security rather than insecurity
and applied for a job with Samhall Work Aid.

You can't get the sack there.

The state set it up
for people who couldn't get work.

You're supposed to have an ailment of some sort
in order to apply to them.

I had my back.

But you can't be ill
and keep up with the work.

When I was up in Sysslebäck
the business was beds.

Our job was to package nine thousand beds a week.

There were six or seven of us on each line.

We were working two lines.

One thing leads to another.

There were sick notes here
and sick notes there.

Eventually there was just one line
but we were supposed to keep the same rate anyway
and produce the same number of beds.

It became too stressful
and that leads to injuries.

See this ganglion cyst.

It's since I worked in packing.

You have to use your wrist too much.

I'm much better
doing what I'm doing now.

We do meal deliveries
on Mondays, Wednesdays and Fridays.

It's for people who aren't able
to make their own meals.

Their minds might be quite sharp
but they still can't manage.

And then there are those who are confused.

Who don't know . . .
Have we had a meal today?

A couple of months ago
the price was fifty-eight kronor.

There was a hell of an outcry
when they put it up to sixty-two.

I do understand them.

If they're living in a flat
pensioners will be liable to pay rent.

If they're living in a house it's usually been paid off.

It's the ones who live in flats who . . .

But when they can't manage
to make their own meals
they don't have a great deal of choice.

If you order pancakes
you don't get jam with them.

You have to buy it yourself.

Think about it now . . .
five or six pancakes
for sixty-two kronor.

Someone from the home help service
will come and help heat them up
so they do get the full service
but it's about the money.

They make the meals in the community hospital.

It lacks seasoning
but that's because
it has to suit everyone.

You can add your own seasoning.

And then of course there's the fact
that the elderly
don't have the faintest idea
what kind of food it is.

Cod with mustard *au gratin* for instance.

What's that?

They've never cooked anything like that
but it's pork and potatoes.

Sometimes you have to sit and explain
what on earth it is.

There are times when I don't understand either.

In spite of the fact I've had an affair with a cook.

You just have to guess.

People aren't used to eating
noodles and all that.

Older people.

What kind of thing is it?

I have to tell them it's spaghetti.

We deliver their food to the fridge.

That way you can see who is eating and who isn't.

Sometimes the dishes haven't been touched.

You have to try to cajole them.

That's your energy sitting there.

You must eat something.

It's a good job
and you get to know people.

It's sad when they pass away
one by one
but it's all part of the job so . . .

You get new clients.

You have to take it as it comes.

We knock
then open the door and shout.

Hello!

Here we are with your meal.

She was lying there in the kitchen.

She'd fallen off a chair
and hurt herself so badly
that . . .

All we could do was call emergency.

That's all we can do.

One day you might be there and . . .
bright as a button.

You go three days later
and no one answers the door.

He's been taken to the community hospital
and doesn't come home again.

It happens so quickly.

So terribly quickly.

My dad was unemployed for a while
then he was sent on a welding course
even though he'd been a welder all his life
but he had to do it
to get the paper qualification.

They moved to Hallstahammar
but I'd dropped out of school in Year Eight
and worked the whole of Year Nine
at an OK petrol station in Enköping
so I told them
you'll just have to move by yourselves.

We'd moved around all my life.

We were small then
so we didn't pay much attention to it.

But I had no wish to move like that.

Too much moving to no purpose.

The people I didn't know
before moving here
they were a bit sceptical about me.

They got it into their heads
I was a Stockholmer.

It's thirty-seven miles
from Enköping to Stockholm
so . . .

Well, I was a Stockholmer anyway.

I had the advantage
that my brothers were already living here.

So when we went to Värmlandsporten
they knew people
even though I didn't know anyone.

The real bugger was
having to ask for a lift.

I wasn't used to that.

I'd been able to take a taxi down to town
or ride my bike and go to the pub
but that wasn't possible here.

I had a hell of a job getting home
when my brothers had already left.

I like it here
I do.

I really didn't think I would
but once I'd come here . . .
I just stuck.

There was still a post office
and Birgit's was open
and the bridge was open.

Now things are closing down bit by bit.

My dad had a stone mason's business.

I'm a qualified stonemason.

I was the first in six generations
who didn't want to take over the family business
even though I was the eldest.

The reason I didn't want to take it over
was that I was born naked and alone
and will die naked and alone
but the bit in between
is mine.

Others shouldn't poke their noses in.

We didn't talk to one another
for a year or more.

Me and my father
and my grandfather.

Those of us who come from Halden
were called the Swedish Reserves in Norway
because there's a lot of Swedish in our language.

We've never regarded Sweden as foreign.

My mother's father was from Gothenburg
and my father's mother from the Bullare district.

My daughter is married in Västerås
and my son's partner
is a girl from Stockholm.

We borderers
are neither Norwegians nor Swedes.

We are borderers.

The company's called Toolmarket Norden.

We produce tools.

Cutting tools and grinding tools.

In Oslo we manufacture mincers and blades
designed for slicing
sausages and burgers.

We produce paper knives for newspapers
for presses
for paper mills.

We sharpen the blades used
for cutting up the logs
used for paper making.

That's done in Ambjörby
in the building that used to be the chipboard factory.

We sharpen blades for sawmills
and manufacture specialist blades.

We make them from steel up here.

That's what we've invested in here.

Norway has suffered deindustrialisation
as a result of the oil.

Industry used to lead the way in terms of wages.

But once the oil industry arrived
that disappeared.

People in the oil industry were so well-paid
that other industries couldn't keep up.

Central and local government sectors
also looked at the oil industry
and made demands based on it.

It's destroyed all of Norway's industries
more or less.

Wage levels became too high.

My employees here
earn substantially more
than when they were with Byggelit
which had the chipboard place up here
or what they earn as building workers.

In spite of that though
you'll still be ten or twelve thousand
a month
below the Norwegian rate.

That's led us
to consider
moving even more things
here from Norway.

I had a shop
at a little place called Kornsjö
on the border between Norway and Sweden.

Swedes used to come across to us and do their shopping
because the Swedish krona was worth a lot more
than the Norwegian.

They used to buy flour, sugar
margarine, cheese
mackerel in tomato sauce and flatbread
just to give some examples.

It was profitable
until nineteen eighty-two
when it came to a complete stop.

They didn't come to do their shopping any more.

It's very quiet here in Osebol
especially in autumn and winter.

It's as if people go into hibernation.

You hardly see anyone at all.

Neither Kari nor I feel the need
to socialise with a lot of people.

We've got a large house, large garden
and we have a cottage.

There's quite enough
to fill our days.

There's a lot of ordinary domestic tasks
cooking, baking bread
pickling herring.

People like us who come from the coast
will happily eat herring five days a week.

I was in Halden yesterday and bought fish pie
and fresh prawns.

Kai Johansen b. 1951
Kari Molteberg b. 1949 | *673*

If war broke out today
it would be easy to cut off
the lifeblood of Sweden, don't you think?

Three bombs
and you've cut off
Malmö, Gothenburg and Stockholm.

Where will they get their food?

How are they supposed to transport food
if they can't get hold of fuel?

People ought to live
where it's possible to grow things.

Norway has done better in that respect.

We've subsidised small-scale farming
to get a better pattern of settlement.

In Norway
there are people still living in the countryside
and running farms.

When I bought this house
I also bought all the books Folke Ekberg left behind
wonderful books.

A first edition of Strindberg.

Dan Andersson
Gustaf Fröding
Knut Hamsun
and any number of volumes of history.

I love reading.

Read the seventh volume of Carl Grimberg
about migration
and you'll understand what's going to happen here.

Muslims and Christians don't go together.

If I was running the country
I wouldn't worry too much about
what happens in Africa and the Middle East.

There's nothing nine or ten million people
can do about that anyway.

I would see to it that Sweden prospered
that's to say, I'd manage what is actually here.

I think we should be paying just as much
to provide work for young Swedes
as for someone from Syria.

Those issues are high on the agenda in Osebol.

People are moving away
there are no jobs.

We are exporting them to other areas.

Those who've had to leave
have lost the right
to live where they want to live.

A lot of people call me a racist.

I'm not a racist.

My aunt is a missionary
who's been in Africa since nineteen sixty-seven.

Along with some others my family
has financed homes for the handicapped down there
and built a school for them.

I think that kind of aid
is completely all right.

Ten years ago we had
one hundred and fifty elk we could shoot
in the hunting zone I belong to.

Last year there were five bulls with under ten points
and seven calves.

I've got hunting rights to two areas
that I haven't been able to rent out
because of the wolves.

There are cottages
that can't be rented to hunters
because of the wolves.

Those of us living in small communities
have to pay for everything
all the costs involved in having wolves.

And who gets any joy out of the wolves?

No one.

Kari and I have seen wolves and bears
many times.

We had a bear no more than a yard in front of the car.

We'd been out to the hotel for lunch
and it ran
straight out in front of the car.

Both sides were fenced off
so it couldn't get away.

Not for a hundred yards or so
and then it disappeared.

When we're out hunting
bears are no problem to the dogs.

They're not a problem.

We can use the forest
along with bears
but we can't use the forest
along with wolves.

I've heard that the turnover
in the shop and petrol station
fell by thirty per cent
after the wolves returned.

Hunters spend a lot of money
during the hunting season
and when they disappear
a small community like this suffers.

The butchery shed we have in Osebol
wouldn't have been built nowadays.

Because of the hunting
we have our own shooting ranges.

But hardly anyone goes there these days.

Hunting was what held small communities together.

I don't believe other kinds of tourism
can replace it.

What other sort of person would be interested
in the forests up here?

In summer
the place is swarming with midges and mosquitoes.

And you get nowhere in the winter
either because there's too little snow
or too much.

People actually interested in nature
don't come here.

They go to other places
that are much more beautiful.

There's nothing particularly special
about the natural scenery here.

I like this place
because it's so quiet
and it's a reasonable distance
from where I come from.

But I wouldn't be living here
if I wanted real nature around me.

I'd have lived in Idre or Särna
places farther north.

Östersund and even farther up.

There's more real nature up there.

The crossroads at Värnäs is
the place with the biggest development potential
in Torsby Rural District.

But the council isn't interested.

Torsby and Sysslebäck are the only places
they are investing in.

But Norra Ny is more central than Sysslebäck.

We ought to link up with Ekshärad instead.

Have a single council district for this ditch . . .
that's what I call this valley.

It's a big ditch.

My grandfather was interviewed
by Aftenposten, Norway's biggest paper,
when he retired.

He was eighty-six at that point.

He was on the board
of the Pentecostal Movement in Norway
and had a stone mason's business
that he passed down to my dad.

When he was asked
if he felt he was highly skilled
he answered
the only thing I know
is that I know very little.

He died at the age of ninety-two.

I sat with him that last night.

He slept for a quarter of an hour
then woke for a quarter of an hour.

He knew he was dying.

The nurse came in.

She washed him
and put his nightshirt on back to front.

Then he woke up.

What's all this?
he said.

Mr Johansen, she said
we put your nightshirt the wrong way round
because we didn't want to wake you.

Well, see about turning it round
he said
I don't want my tie hanging down my back.

That was two hours before he died.

That attitude
of sticking to the way things should be
regardless of how you feel.

I miss that in people.

A kind of moral code.

During the years we were in Stockholm . . .
you waste so much energy unnecessarily there.

The last straw was
the time I had a meeting at two o'clock.

It took two hours to get there.

Then I should have got home
in no more than an hour.

He picked me up at four o'clock
instead of three o'clock
because he was sitting in a queue of traffic.

And it took us three hours to get home.

There were two car accidents.

I just . . .
no, this is not on.

I was out the whole day
for a one-hour meeting.

It was a sign.

We had to do something.

Friends who live closer to the city said
move here.

But I don't get on in cities.

I was working with loads of people.

I wanted to go into the forest
like now
and get my energy back.

It was really lovely and quiet in Tyresö
but the commuting took up
so much time.

We lived in that house for eight years
and the neighbours
it was never more than hello there
sometimes not even that
because they move house and are off
move and are off.

No one had any desire or energy
to meet new people.

But I'm open to doing that.

I like to chat
and make contact
and meet new people.

Sometimes when I was driving to work
I'd leave a bit earlier.

I didn't like that long stream
and everyone with their . . .
like robots.

One direction in the morning.

The other direction in the evening.

I'd buy a coffee and a roll
and stand and watch it all
and I felt no
I don't want to be like this.

Loads of people everywhere
on the underground and the busses
but all of them shut in
and wanting to be in their own worlds.

Leaving gaps of fifteen feet
at the bus stop
if possible.

You just get weary.

You have to live.

You have to be earning money all the time.

694 | *Natia Ellelund b. 1988*

My family had known István for a long time.

Ruslan moved in with me in Torsby
and started to work for him.

I finished at the Stjerne School
got a trainee placement with the TV in Stockholm
and stayed there and worked.

It was in make-up.

So I did two seasons of Let's Dance
two seasons of the Battle of the Choirs
one season of Stars on Ice.

We moved to Stockholm in two thousand and eight.

We moved together.

Last autumn István mentioned
he might need me up here.

There were orders coming in all the time.

It didn't take much thinking about.

He also said there was somewhere to live.

That was a major problem
about moving to Värmland.

Finding a job and somewhere to live at the same time.

It was almost more impossible
to get a flat in Karlstad
than in Stockholm.

We joined the queue
and registered our interest in lots of different places
but were never called to a viewing.

Ruslan Ellelund b. 1986

In Stockholm people move.

You never know
who used to live here or
what happened in the flat
and there's no one you can ask.

Here everyone knows.

People know stories about the house
and who has owned it.

I used to come and do some shopping here.

I can still remember
coming in here
and buying food.

In some ways
it feels a bit strange.

They are making it more difficult for people
to live in villages.

Everyone wants to move to cities.

It's maybe easier
to manipulate people there.

It feels as if you have more freedom
in small places.

But you get a feeling
that the government is doing everything
to get people to move
to the big cities.

You end up a bit like zombies.

You get trapped in that
I must, I must.

Natia Ellelund b. 1988 | 699

They close the schools
move everyone to Torsby
which is half an hour's drive.

I'd live here, no doubt about that,
but when she's bigger
I've no idea how to make it work.

Commute, sure
but we might want her to attend
gymnastics courses or dance courses
or courses in painting.

But unfortunately all of that's been moved
to bigger places.

Why I don't know
since there are still
people with children here.

Many people think . . .
or it seems that they do
that it's easier in big cities.

Everything lies close by
and it feels easier.

But in reality
if you compare things
it isn't any easier there at all.

I moved away from here
when I left school.

When I was nineteen or thereabouts.

I had a flat in Stöllet.

Then Grandad was left on his own.

I was on my own then too.

He couldn't take care of things all alone
so I moved back home
lived upstairs
and looked after the house.

Grandma and Grandad hadn't done anything
so everything dated from sixty-seven.

I've had to keep at it the whole time.

Not a single window or anything had been changed.

So everything fell on me.

All his income went on lorries.

That's where it all ended up.

The house
was of no importance.

I've always liked it here.

There's a sense of security.

Natural in a kind of way.

I don't get on anywhere else . . .
it has to be here.

Things went quite well in Stöllet
they did
but I've never really liked
living in flats.

I need a bit of freedom
beyond the walls.

The community isn't
what it used to be.

Not like when there was the shop
and local people still here.

It was a kind of meeting place
where everyone talked to everyone.

It's not like that anymore.

I miss Alf at Byggninga
and Henry at Törnsgårn and Staffan.

No one's left, like.

From the moment the shop went
you never see them.

There'd always be someone at the shop.

Urban Nilsson b. 1976 | *707*

They got an EU grant to repair the bridge
but the local authority backed out.

Wouldn't pay their share
and they had to give the grant back.

It was all because of the local authority.

It would have been repaired otherwise.

It was devastating for Osebol
when the bridge closed.

Now you've no choice but to use this dirt road
and it's full of potholes.

I really don't understand
why it isn't considered a kind of cultural issue.

It's the only two-arched bridge around.

There isn't another.

I'm a digger driver at the moment.

I used to have a lorry, too, but I sold it last autumn.

It's extremely difficult to get a job here.

They favour outsiders
and that's sad.

Come the end
I was the only one with a gritter lorry
in quite a long stretch of the valley.

Eventually I got sick of it.

They'd rather get a lorry from Ekshärad
than take one that's here.

I mean
keeping these things on your farm
doesn't come cost free.

You can't just carry on doing so endlessly.

I was in Torsby today
driving a wheel loader for the haulage depot.

I've been there six weeks at a stretch now
covering for the holiday.

I unload the heavy trucks when they come in
and drive shovels of grit out to customers.

And load the trailers that come in
and then maybe see about grading the grit.

It's hard going.

At times I have more than enough
at others nothing at all.

Spreading things out evenly is hard
which is why it's very difficult to say no.

You can find yourself working seven days a week
for I don't know how long
because you know there might be nothing
for weeks on end.

I've worked as a nursing assistant
but eventually it became impossible.

My body said that's enough.

So now I'm what I call
a housewife living a life of luxury
or something like that.

I have fibromyalgia and ADHD.

That's how it played out.

My mind was running flat out
and my body couldn't manage.

I had to take things easier.

A bit.

It gets boring sometimes
but there's plenty to do at home.

I've got that fellow there
that I take for a walk in the morning.

Then it's the usual
cleaning, washing, tidying up
cooking and seeing it's all done
when they arrive home.

Everything neat and tidy
and suddenly it's evening.

You have routines
otherwise you'd go crazy.

If I was going to move
I'd move somewhere in this area.

This is where I feel happy.

I wouldn't be happy in Torsby.

Mainly because I had to go there
to finish comprehensive school
and couldn't attend here.

I had to go there in Year Nine.

                                        I feel sorry for them.

                                        Away for twelve hours.

                          Completely exhausted – it's not human.

As soon as I got a driving licence
I took the car every day I could.

That way I could get to school
and we'd have two lessons
and I'd be finished.

Otherwise I'd have to sit for four, five hours
waiting for the bus
and that really gets to you.

Kattis Nilsson b. 1996
Urban Nilsson b. 1976 | 713

They should have kept the small schools.

Yes, I think they get a lot of their priorities all wrong.

Which we find irritating, obviously.

They're cutting back on everything
but when it comes to refugees
there's always money available
however much it may be.

Of course, you can't say that
if you do you're a racist the moment you open your mouth.

I really don't think I am, though.

Because they won't run any schools
or care for the elderly or anything else.

I think the prioritisation is completely wrong
because basically
all that money comes from our people.

They can say what they like but that's a fact.

It may not be from the same account
but it all comes from the taxpayers, doesn't it?

Anna Nilsson b. 1972
714 | Urban Nilsson b. 1976

There were twelve of us in my class
when I was at Stöllet
and then we split up.

Ten of us had passed maths
when we were at Stöllet.

One had a pass in maths
when we passed out of the Fryken School in Torsby.

Joining a class for one year
the last year
when they've all been together since Year Five or Six
isn't easy.

And going to a new school
new teachers, new people
everything is new.

I got on really well in my class
but ooh lordie lordie.

I don't know how often I sat and cried
in the first weeks
because I didn't want to go to school.

I didn't want to.

If I hadn't been helped
by these two here
I wouldn't have gone to school
at all.

The council didn't give Stöllet any sort of priority.

The last few years they didn't even have competent teachers.

So when they started in Torsby
they weren't at anything like the same level
as the pupils there.

They had a huge struggle
trying to catch up.

My grades just crashed.

It makes you feel
as if you know nothing
even though you'd believed
you knew something.

Urban Nilsson b. 1976
Kattis Nilsson b. 1996 | *717*

I was so happy when I graduated from school this past spring
thank God for that

I felt that, well, I've got through that.

Struggled and won through, sort of.

These two pushed me all the time.

There were many days when I said
I just can't manage
I don't give a damn about it.

They'd say something
and so . . . well
I'll give it another go
and so it went on.

They've just been there
and said things will work out
it's OK
it'll soon be over.

That's what you have to remember
that it'll soon be over.

It means a lot of ferrying about.

You're happy to do it, of course
but driving a car doesn't come cheap these days.

You're taking on a sizeable financial load
to make life easier for youngsters.

> I spent the whole of my student grant
> buying fuel
> to get there
> and to get back home.

That's it
it makes you so bloody angry
that they don't realise
that some pupils have a long way to travel.

Given that everything's on the internet these days
they could have stated the night before
that tomorrow's classes are cancelled
but they didn't do that
so they turned up
and found they didn't have any lessons.

So much of it was just stupid, I thought.

Urban Nilsson b. 1976
Kattis Nilsson b. 1996 | 719

Take me
I chose the Transport programme in Säffle
and the first timetable we got
said we should attend Monday to Friday.

Many of us were from Torsby
and we said that it's so bloody far for us
to go home for the weekend
that we'll include Fridays in it.

And we were allowed to do it.

They understood completely.

Their suggestion was
she should stay over
at a friend's place in Torsby
and sleep there.

Kattis said
Forget it, I'm going home
I've got animals at home.

Urban Nilsson b. 1976
720 | *Anna Nilsson b. 1972*

Whatever the situation
I don't think teenagers should just be left to drift.

You want to know they're being fed
that they're sleeping at night
and getting up in the morning.

That's just the way of it.

Heads with some level of competence would be good.

And they need to prioritise
something more than the Torsby centre.

        And more than the ski pupils at the Stjerne School.

Small schools are best of all.

They usually produce good people.

You don't get all the crap
you get in a big school.

> In Stöllet we were like a little family
> and then I went to Torsby.

> Torsby isn't far away
> but they all hated each other there.

> There were different classes, A, B, C and D.

Urban Nilsson b. 1976
722 | *Kattis Nilsson b. 1996*

I think there were twenty-six of us.

When you're in a class that big
the teacher doesn't have time
so pupils who are finding it a bit harder
don't get the help they need.

They might find it embarrassing
to raise their hands to say
I haven't understood again . . .

I found maths really difficult
but I didn't get the help I needed.

Many, many times
I thought back to Stöllet School
and thought what it would have been like
if I'd stayed there
throughout.

Unless they change some things
and prioritize differently
rural communities are going to die out.

That's a fact.

Drive through Stöllet on a Saturday evening
it's deserted.

It's dead.

The council owned a lot of grassy areas.

They used to be properly looked after and nice.

They look bloody awful now, to be blunt.

And the council has sold off just about everything else . . .
blocks of flats and so on.

Most people just grin and bear it.

That's all.

And we've got no idea what to do.

It's easy to sit at the kitchen table like this
and say one thing or another
but it doesn't go beyond that.

People are unwilling to say what they think
or show they want to do something
because they're afraid of what others will think.

Afraid of falling out with people.

What's said is that this family has been active here for centuries
so they must know best.

Anything beyond that is a no-no.

Coming from somewhere else
I can see things differently.

Maybe they want to lord it over everyone else
rather than listen to their neighbours
and try to work together
to make it a better place to live.

Urban Nilsson b. 1976
Anna Nilsson b. 1972 | *725*

I'm convinced the time will come
when people get sick of living on top of one another
and will come back out to the countryside.

I doubt I'll live to see it
but I do believe things will change.

When I'm in Stockholm, like
I get so unbelievably stressed
I don't know where I am.

The bloody traffic and that.

And everyone in a hurry.

Karlstad's all right.

I wouldn't want anywhere bigger than that.

It was built in eighteen sixty-nine
but there was a house here before that.

Above Åke Axelsson's
and a little to the north
there's a red house.

It's half the old house.

A lake they called Svinsjön forms there in spring
when there's a flood.

They floated the house down
and carried it up
and erected it at Tômta.

My grandfather bought this place in eighteen ninety-six.

He was from Kullberget.

That's over beyond Järnbergsås.

It's a croft.

Then he moved down here
and got together with Kerstin at Törnsgårn.

Do you remember Axel?

Axel at Törnsgårn?

It was his sister.

Then they bought this place.

This house used to be up there.

Other side of the cypress.

I moved it in seventy-six.

Here's the old one.

That's what it looked like.

Grandad had renovated it.

This was taken nineteen hundred and two.

There's a small child sitting there.

That's Annie at Sandvik
she's the one who married Daniel.

She was born in nineteen hundred.

She's two years old there.

I took it down and rebuilt it here.

It was in a poor position.

In the shade and the ground was poor.

All the women
were housewives
and all the men
worked in forestry.

There's no one now
in Osebol
working in forestry.

In a way it's good.

Everything they did
the whole winter
maybe sixty woodsmen, here in Osebol
was all manual work.

They didn't have chainsaws
or anything else.

A chap
sitting in his machine
in patent leather shoes
can get all that done
in a day.

They had cabins out in the forest
and they'd stay out there for a week.

Up to a fortnight
if it was a long way.

Took food with them
and horses.

It was no fun in the winter.

With maybe six feet of snow.

Not easy to get to.

They used saws
to fell the trees
and axes
to lop the branches
and a barking spade
to bark the logs.

After that along came
a two-man team
with a horse and sledge
and hauled it out.

Chainsaws came in in the fifties
and agricultural tractors with chains
that were used in the forests.

They fell more trees now
than they used to.

There's a much bigger market.

At that time they didn't use to have
the resources to fell very much.

I don't know how many timber lorries
pass here every day.

They didn't use to use lorries.

They'd haul it down here to the river
from the forest.

Then they would float it.

Osebol meadow was used for stacking timber.

Nineteen seventy-three.

My dad had a building firm.

We worked together
he and me.

We built a purification plant
and a sewage works
in Fastnäs
but at this stage
I was helping ABV at Krusmon.

They were in a great hurry
building the chipboard factory.

One evening
the twenty-third of January.

When I came home
I had a slight temperature and felt shivery.

I had something to eat
and went off to bed.

A car pulled up outside
and someone came rushing in.

It was Folke Hagström.

Where's Alvar?

He's not well, she said.

He had something to eat
and went to bed.

Well, no point
in beating about the bush
he said.

Birger's been in a crash
down in Gravol.

He's still in the car
but he's wheezing and rattling.

I leapt up
into the car
and off.

So I was, well . . .

There was no one there . . .

Well, the truck driver . . .

A few cars had passed
but none of them had stopped.

I went and tried to feel his pulse
but it was already too late.

My mother moved up to Dalby
then
up to her mother's.

I had to take over everything.

Construction jobs
and getting everything finished
and . . .

I didn't have any plans
to carry on
but . . .

What had happened was
that down beyond Björkebo Campsite
before Gravol . . .

There's a little red house
on the left-hand side
coming from here
and there's also a concrete wall.

He was coming from Fastnäs
and there was a lorry
that had driven from Örebro.

Delivering Ytong blocks
up to the chipboard factory
and it was sleeting.

An old fellow
called Johan
was living on the other side of the road there.

He was out walking.

The lorry driver didn't want to splash him
and moved out.

There was a car behind him
that witnessed it all.

He moved out onto the left-hand side
as my dad was coming from the south.

He swerved his truck
sharply back in
and the trailer swung out.

Before the collision
my dad ran into the wall
trying to get out of the way.

It was dark, of course.

You could see the marks.

And then the trailer's bogie wheels
swung in and hit the whole car

It wasn't his fault
though that's not much comfort.

Nineteen seventy-eight.

I had the caravan up in Tandådal
and Henke started to take an interest
in downhill skiing.

A club started training
on one of the hills there.

They had a rope tow
a petrol-driven one.

I took a look at it
and thought
see that bugger.

What if I bought one like that
and found a slope?

Because at that time
there was only Ekshärad.

When I got home
I told István
I was going to buy
a petrol-driven ski tow.

Good idea, he said.

I'll come in with you.

A week passed.

And István rang.

Have you ordered that tow yet?

No, I haven't got a price yet.

That's good, he said
because I've just bought a tow.

You've bought a tow?

Yes, I bought the old rope tow from Långberget.

God in heaven!

It's big.

We'll need to put in electricity
and have a bigger slope.

Yeah, yeah, we'll fix that
we'll fix that.

The optimist, see.

I talked to Bengt Sonesson about the ground.

Yes, of course, no problem.

Everyone turned out.

Became members.

Old women became members.

At our best we had four hundred members
in a village as small as this.

I took ill this past April.

I went down to the cellar
to load the washing machine
and I was so bloody dizzy my head was spinning.

That's the last thing I remember.

Ulrika tried to call me a thousand times.

She rang István.

Have you seen Dad?

He came here and had a look round.

My car was at home
the door was open
and the cat was running in and out yowling.

You'll have to look for him
she said.

They went in and searched the place.

And I was lying there on the floor
in the washhouse.

My body temperature
was twenty-six degrees
and I had pressure sores.

I'd been lying there
three and a half days.

The helicopter ambulance picked me up
and took me to Karlstad.

Once there I was put on a respirator.

I wouldn't have lasted
many more hours.

When István tried to open
the washhouse door
something had been
in the way.

It was me lying against the door.

It was a bit like that with Jon Halvardsson.

The one who lived up there in the stables.

Tore and Ulla-Britt were living
in that house that burned down.

I was going up to their place one evening.

It was dark
and as I was passing Jon's
I heard
Oh, oh.

I went over
opened the door
and he fell out.

He'd been sitting leaning on the door.

He had a burst appendix
and peritonitis.

He was the one who built Nystugan.

The one who owned all of it.

He was a drinker and used to act as guarantor for people.

In the end he went bankrupt.

He lived in poverty.

He would never go up to Sundholm
and do his own shopping.

He wanted me to go
and do the shopping for him.

I'd get twenty-five öre for my trouble.

Twenty-five öre was a lot of money
in those days.

There's a chap who rents it . . .
well, he gets a subsidy.

An EU subsidy.

He looks after the land and ploughs it
which is really good.

We don't get a return on it.

It's just that it gets looked after.

Otherwise it'd become overgrown.

It's not possible
to make a profit on it.

People up here . . .
the only way they had of getting food
was wild animals
and what they could take from their fields.

Every square yard was important.

That's why they had shielings
where they let the animals out in the summer.

I often think about it . . .
Grandma and Grandad
were living in Hemgårn then
along with four children
and servants.

Two maids and a couple of farmhands
and they all had to be fed
on what they could get out of it.

I have a big field by Åke's place.

East of there.

That's where the girls grazed their horse.

I used to say this
to the girls
because the paddock for the horse
was never big enough for them.

I said
they had working horses
they had cows and sheep
and Grandma and Grandad
and farm servants
and children
and it was big enough then.

But now it's not big enough
for one horse.

I was the first person round here
to buy a video camera.

István would borrow it
whenever anything was on.

He filmed the Osebol market at the start.

Most of those in it
are long gone now.

My grandma was still alive
at the time I bought the camera.

I went up to visit her
and I put it on a stand
and set it going.

It was the kind
that had a VHS cassette.

She talked and talked
and then we went indoors.

I turned on the TV
and connected up the camera
and she sat
and watched herself.

But . . .
who can see this?

She had a cousin in Uggenäs
a cousin called Märta.

Is Märta in Uggenäs watching?

I've still got the film.

It's just like when she was alive.

I made a recording from T V.

It was all about the Osebol bridge.

About closing it.

They'd been up in the shop
filming customers.

Almost all of them are gone.

Vilhelm, Per-Erik's father
he was filmed at Osebol market.

He was selling carrots.

There's hardly anyone
who remembers him
or what he looked like.

Having them on moving film
is worthwhile.

The worst thing is
not to have given more thought to the future.

Someone like Axel . . .
I spent a lot of time with him
in my early teens.

He talked and talked.

And Helmer at Eftnäs
he was someone who knew everything
from generations back.

If we could just bring them back.

There's so much we don't know.

When I've had
my boys with me in the forest
I tell them
this bit is called this
this bit is called that
and this bit of forest
belongs to so-and-so.

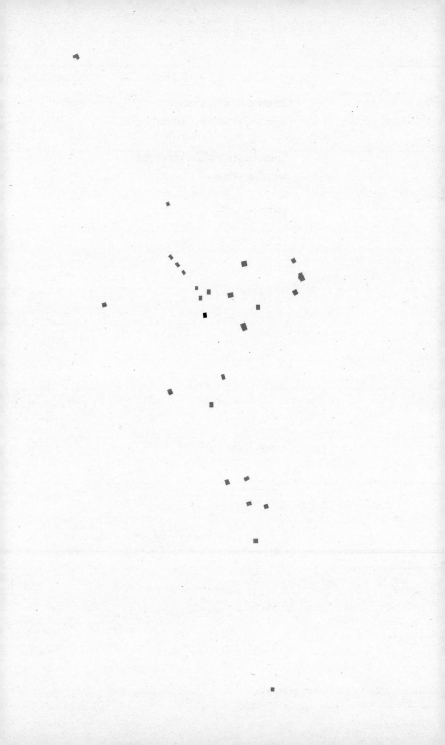

In my country, Hungary
there is almost no winter.

Sometimes it's just very cold
without snow.

I need winter.

I had a good life in Hungary.

I had a good salary
I had good friends.

But several of my friends
not just one
died in accidents.

One fell from a cliff
it was an avalanche.

One day I just I woke up and . . .
oh God
I'm all alone.

I'm divorced too
so there are a lot of things.

And I don't like
the Hungarian people's mentality.

Not all of them of course
but many of the people living in Hungary
are not very nice people.

They think they're the best.

That people who don't have posh expensive cars
are just shit.

They're extremely materialistic.

And they aren't rich.

They buy expensive cars
gold chains and watches
but there's almost nothing behind it
and not much IQ.

Country people in Hungary
are still nice
but there's fewer and fewer of them.

I won't be going back to Hungary.

Things are good here.

I was involved in a climbing accident once.

I broke my leg.

So it can be dangerous.

Ninety percent of all climbing accidents
result from people making mistakes.

Belays being placed in the wrong place
or forgetting to lock a carabiner.

Ten percent are not caused by people.

A rock falls
or ice falls.

Or an avalanche.

But ninety percent are your own fault.

But it's not important.

Maybe there's a huge book
in which everyone's life is written.

How and when he or she will die.

If I'm going to die next year while climbing . . .
I'm not afraid.

There's always something
that might turn out badly.

I might die
if I go out when it's slippery.

I might die
in a car accident
or a plane crash.

I think life in town is more dangerous
than up a mountain.

I've talked with Äke
about this.

We feel fortunate
to be living here
not in Stockholm
or Gothenburg.

Not in big cities.

We still have security here.

We aren't close to terrorists.

What happened in Stockholm
was dreadful.

It's exactly the same
as in France and Germany.

It's a new world.

I lived in Budapest too long.

I was in the police.

We'd been given special training
and had cars, automatic weapons
grenades, bulletproof vests.

Our job was to protect ministers.

My job was to drive the car
and if anything happened
protect the passenger
and try to wipe out the terrorists.

At night, sometimes,
we'd drive to a park
where people had been murdered
with automatic weapons
five minutes earlier.

But I never had to fire my gun.

I worked as a policeman for seven, almost eight, years.

But since the police didn't earn very much money
there was a lot of corruption.

The first level was down on the street.

If you drove too fast and the police stopped you . . .
no problem.

Two thousand, that's all
and you're allowed to drive off.

Sometimes there was corruption higher up.

What often happened was
that we'd arrested known criminals.

Maybe not terrorists but mafia.

We'd be over the moon.

Twenty-four hours later
they'd be walking out of the police station.

Someone had received a couple of hundred thousand kronor.

I got tired of it.

Another thing.

I'm quite a kind man.

Fining people wasn't that important to me.

But that's what mattered most to the Hungarian police.

Get out on the street and issue fines
to bring in money for the police.

I had a lot of arguments with my superiors.

It was a terrible world.

It's not a failure of the system.

It's the people.

Many people became millionaires
after communism.

That's true in many countries.

There was harsh oppression
and then it was lifted.

Everyone could do everything.

There were no rules
nothing
just money.

I still have many Hungarian friends.

Hungary is a great destination if you're a tourist.

Fine cities, friendly people.

Hungary has a good side
but its other side is awful.

I don't watch Hungarian TV
or anything Hungarian on Facebook.

I've put all that behind me.

For the first two years
I wasn't sure
if I'd stay here in Sweden.

I like Norway too
but there's too much rain.

It's beautiful
it's an amazing country
but living here is much better.

Nature is kinder.

You see forests that are green.

In Norway there's nothing but water and rocks.

Levi Stenberg b. 1973 | 775

And the people.

OK, the people in Skåne are a bit odd.

They're nice people.

I never have problems with people.

Not with Swedish people.

But I don't think they're so close to one another in Skåne.

They keep their distance.

People up here are different.

It's a mix, of course.

But I think people are friendlier here.

It's easier to make friends.

If I need help
they'll help me
and if they need help
I'll help them.

It works.

If I'm not at home
people keep an eye on the house.

It's like . . . not a family
but it's going that way.

Wages in Hungary are very low
and prices are very high.

It's out of balance.

I lived in Norway for six months
roughly two years ago
before I bought this house
Sandvik.

It's incredibly expensive there
but there's a balance.

Wages are high enough to live on.

Wages in Hungary are too low.

Lots of people are leaving Hungary.

The population is getting smaller and smaller.

Here people are leaving the small villages
and moving closer to the cities
or into the cities.

In Hungary that doesn't work
because there aren't enough jobs for everyone.

Now I will tell you something.

A couple of years ago
I did a two-week ski tour
along the Kungsleden trail up north.

I started from Abisko
and skied down to the Kebnekajse
and back towards Kiruna and . . .

It was very strange.

I came across a little Sami village
just eight houses or so.

The Sami only used it in the summer.

I got a special feeling.

Something happened in my mind.

I sat down
looked at the village and said
Oh my God
I lived here
three or four hundred years ago.

It was like . . .
what's the French word . . .
déjà vu.

It was very strange.

I felt I'd been born there
or had lived there
hundreds of years ago.

After that I decided
right, I will live here in Sweden.

I have swapped lives.

Someone down here asked me
Where do you come from?

My answer was
my body comes from Hungary
and my soul from Norrland.

We've driven into elk twice
Alf and me.

But we survived.

The first time was in Ljusnästorp.

We'd been over west in Fensbol
helping out with the haymaking
and were driving to have a look
where they were building a bridge farther north
to see how far they'd got . . .
Likenäs bridge, I think it was.

Arne was little then.

Sitting in the back seat.

No child seats or anything
in those days.

And an elk comes
down a slope
and up over the radiator.

The windscreen shattered in a thousand bits.

The elk thumped to the ground.

Alf was about to get out
and try to kill it.

But it got up
gave itself a shake
and ran off.

Early on when I came here
there was a real sewing circle.

We worked, did embroidery.

We were scattered around here and there
took it in turns to hold the sewing circle.

What happened then
was that younger ones joined
and older ones passed away.

All except me.

On one occasion Ingalill said
Since no one wants to do any needlework
what about playing bingo
Jon Ola has a set.

All of us were in favour of that.

We haven't started now since Christmas
because it's been so cold.

But otherwise there are eight of us.

We were the ones who helped
and made things for the auction in the school hall.

All the money went to Stödalen.

You wanted it to work out, you did.

Birgit was a driving force
so was Tage.

When I go there
I think it's so empty without Tage.

He used to be sitting there on the sofa
when you entered.

Take down that calendar.

You can see there what I have.

I have that to live for.

Though I don't believe it sometimes.

There's my little lass.

She's got Arne's smile.

It was seven years ago now.

Alf in March and Arne in June.

Three months later I was having a colostomy.

No one thought I'd pull through.

But I did pull through.

I sit at the table here
doing crosswords and reading
and when my back hurts too much
I lie down on the sofa.

I make a bit of food for myself
and try to wash and keep myself clean
and I've managed well enough so far.

I don't want to go into Klarastrand.

I sit down with the TV
at six o'clock
and sit there
until I go to bed
at nine or half past.

I press one button after another
all the channels.

Kisselina sits on my lap
and we just sit there.

I'll watch anything at all.

The news.

And I play bingo
with Ingvar Oldsberg.

I like to keep up
so I know what's happening in the world.

There's a ladder leaning on the south wall
goes up to the chimney.

The weather was so good
I took my walking frame
and went out to pick up the post.

I went round the house
and there were some wood anemones.

I thought I'll pick some
but my head went all dizzy
and I banged my arm on the ladder.

Then the alarm went.

I tried
time after time.

I thought
it doesn't help.

I tried to crawl, to crawl.

At last a lass came.

And they got me up.

They X-rayed it
and it had been pushed up in the joint . . .
the bone had.

There was nothing to be done.

It had to be left to heal as it was.

This shoulder is much higher
than the other.

It never got better.

Certain movements
make it hurt so much.

But I have to accept it.

It's just a trifle really.

Just a trifle.

It was such a fine afternoon.

I was feeling so well
that something was bound to happen.

Sometimes I think it would be better
if I took a flat in Torsby.

But then I want to stay in Osebol too.

That's where I've lived.

It's a long time since you saw bullfinches, isn't it?

There were five or six of them outside here just now.

When winter's at its coldest
there's often fifty or sixty of them.

The birches over there are full of them then.

It's so beautiful
when there's rime-frost on the branches.

They sit there getting warm
when the sun rises.

They're just like red apples.

AFTERWORD

Where does something start? And where does it finish? If it's a fact that the molecules in a body never really stay still, where do I end and where does the space around me begin?

My time in Osebol began one day at the end of September 1970. Dad had got a job at Klarälvdalen Folk High School in Stöllet, a couple of miles north of Osebol on the other side of the river. He and Mum were able to rent the upper floor of Byggninga in Osebol, the same farm where Karin and Alf Håkansson lived. I'd been born three weeks earlier in the maternity ward in Malung. Mum was twenty-three and Dad would be thirty-two that October. My sister was born a year later, my brother seven years later.

My time in Osebol finished several times. First when I moved to Torsby to attend the upper secondary school and only come home at weekends. Then when I moved to Stockholm to study. I lived with Mum and Dad for the summer of 1992 before getting a job as a local reporter with Värmlands Folkblad in Torsby. In 1994 I moved from Torsby to Karlstad and in 1998 to Gothenburg where I still live.

In 2007 my time in Osebol finished once again. Dad was suffering from Alzheimer's and couldn't live at home any longer. In January he moved into a home for dementia sufferers and that summer Mum sold the house she and Dad had built in 1975 on the hill above Karin and Alf.

Today, when I stand on the gravel road that runs past the house and look towards it, it feels as if I still live there. Osebol has grown to be part of me. It's only there that the horizon is in its right place.

From the depths of my heart I want to thank all the people who now live in Osebol. They have shared their time, their lives and their words for this book about Osebol. I interviewed them during 2016 and 2017 and a special thought goes to those who have left us since. Karin, Eivor, Hans, Bror, Lars and Ingalill – I am happy that you are part of this book. Since I did the interviews, five of the people I interviewed have become parents for the first time or again. Christer's daughter Eira, Mattias's daughter Maria, Petra's sons Pontus and Philip, and Natia's and Ruslan's son Milian, Mika's brother, all have Osebol as an important place in their young lives.

The water gleams and the trees grow, in Osebol as in other places. The sun appears to be moving across the sky, though we are the ones who are moving.

Once we were all here and nowhere else.

The interviews were carried out with the support of the Helge Ax:son Johnson Foundation. The work was also supported by Håks Per Persson's Testamentary Foundation.

The interview with Johnny Munk Laursen was conducted in Danish, that with Annemarie den Heijer and Rick Keulen in English; the interview with Kai Johansen and Kari Molteberg was partially conducted in Norwegian, and an interview with Levi Stenberg was conducted in English.